GIFTS FROM BEYOND

GIFTS FROM BEYOND

REFLECTIONS ON INTERRELIGIOUS DIALOGUE AND COLLABORATION

EDITED BY EDWARD E. THOMPSON

Friendship Press™

Gifts from Beyond

Reflections on Interreligious Dialogue and Collaboration

ISBN: 978-1-961088-45-0

Table of Contents

Foreword

Vashti Murphy McKenzie

There is a table that has been set for a long time now, and the National Council of the Churches of Christ in the USA (NCC) has never stopped walking toward it. It is the Interreligious Relations and Collaboration Convening Table.

We forget, sometimes, how long the road has been. In 1943, in the smoke of a world at war, the churches of our forerunner, the Federal Council of Churches, dared to speak of Six Pillars of Peace, as if peace were architecture, something built rather than merely hoped for. In 1951, still shadowed by that same war's aftermath, they spoke again of nurturing relationships with communities of other faiths as central to the work of building Christian unity and integrity in NCC's efforts for peace and human development.

In 1977, NCC turned its gaze toward the United Nations and asked its own government to take seriously the audacious idea that the nations of the earth might be accountable to one another. And by the century's turn, they understood what the prophets always knew: that peace is not the absence of conflict but the presence of justice. Justice is not self-executing. It requires pillars such as faith, peace, advocacy, economics, law, human rights, and ecology. Each discipline is a promise kept or broken in the daily work of nations and neighborhoods alike.

In 1999, the churches stated plainly what they had long practiced imperfectly: building Christian unity and peace among nations could not be separated from building right relationships with Buddhists, Hindus, Jews, Muslims, Sikhs, and others who, in their own tongues, kneel before mystery. Twenty years later, as the nation grew more anxious, divided, and in some places more dangerous for people of many faiths, strangers, and those deemed different, NCC said it again with even greater urgency.

This is the truth this book bears witness to: that the work of the wider peace and the work of the nearer neighbor are, in the end, one work. Martin Luther King Jr. understood it when he insisted that we are caught in an inescapable network of mutuality, tied in a single garment of destiny. What threatens justice anywhere threatens it everywhere. Is it now possible that what heals the wound of division in one relationship begins to heal it in all?

The pillars of peace and the tables of dialogue are not two projects. They are the same house, built from two directions, meeting somewhere in the middle where humility lives.

Gifts from Beyond: Reflections on Interreligious Dialogue and Collaboration underscores the importance of NCC's commitment to dialogue and peace for years and its continued commitment in the future. Special thanks to all of the contributors; the editor, the Very Rev. Dr. Edward E. Thompson; associate editors Barbara G. Hager, Kah-Jin Jeffrey Kuan, Peter E. Makari, and Don Thorsen; Brian Sigmon, CEO of our own Friendship Press; and all who serve on the NCC's Interreligious Relations and Collaboration Convening Table.

Preface

Edward E. Thompson

How well do you know your neighbors who are shaped by religious traditions other than Christianity? What do you know of the traditions in which they live? What might you gain from deeper engagement with your interreligious neighbors, and how would you begin? What kinds of dialogue and collaboration across religions might already be happening in your community, and where would you even start to look? Why should any of these questions matter to you? These are some of the questions that the authors who have contributed to this anthology can help you to answer.

The contributors to this anthology are people connected in various ways to the focus of the National Council of Churches (NCC) on interreligious dialogue and collaboration. Lay and ordained, some have staff positions within their own denominations that put them in charge of interreligious relations. Others are academics working in theology, biblical studies, or specifically in the interreligious arena. Most are members of the Interreligious Relations (IRR) Convening Table and take part in at least one of the five dialogues organized by the NCC in collaboration with other religious bodies. The dialogues take place in bilateral meetings between Christians and adherents of another tradition: Jews, Muslims, Hindus, Buddhists, or Sikhs. Participants in these dialogues are often intrigued to learn of the internal diversity within the other tradition. The chapters draw from these dialogues but also go much deeper into individual experience—in some cases lifelong—with interreligious work.

This collection is meant for a general readership. However, this should not be confused with a lack of expertise, as the authors' bios show. We hope that even those with expertise in interreligious work will find much of value in these contributions. All of the authors have passion for this type of effort and are informed by personal experience with it. Beyond sharing our efforts, we want more people to experience the transformative power and promise of interreligious relationship and collaboration.

The chapters are grouped into four sections, based loosely on the organizing principle or theme of each. These sections were not predetermined. The contributions often overlap the divisions, and the sections are only meant as a hint for how and where you might want to begin reading. The first section, "Growth and Healing," draws together four contributions that focus on deep relationship. Other contributions certainly draw on important relationships, but there is a certain vulnerability infusing these essays which sets them apart. The second section, "Gifts and Challenges," collects five contributions that give summaries of what has come from personal and professional experience through interreligious relations. The third section, "Speaking from Our Traditions," shares similarities with the prior section; but here, the contributors make a clear effort to reflect on interreligious engagement based on the wisdom of their respective traditions within Christianity. The fourth and final section, "Pathways for Living," offers frameworks for living in an interreligious world. All the contributions speak to living well in an interreligious world; but the contributions grouped here are more formal and not based in a specific Christian tradition. Again, there is overlap and the sectional divisions are meant merely as guideposts for beginning.

In addition to the members of the NCC's Interreligious Relations Convening Table who have offered chapters, two of our contributors have served both the NCC and their Christian affiliative bodies at the highest levels. Bishop Elizabeth Eaton, formerly Presiding Bishop of the Evangelical Lutheran Church in America (ELCA), served as Chair of the Governing Board of the NCC in 2024 and 2025. His Eminence Archbishop Elpidophoros, Primate of the Greek Orthodox Church of America, is the current Chair of the Governing Board, having begun his term this year. Bishop Eaton and Archbishop Elpidophoros have provided unique, high-level perspectives on interreligious efforts also grounded in their personal commitments, and we are grateful for their contributions.

We are grateful as well for the contribution of the Foreword by Bishop Vashti McKenzie, President and General Secretary of the National Council of Churches. It was Bishop McKenzie who moved the IRR Convening Table to act on the desire to share the fruits of the NCC's interreligious dialogues and collaboration with the broader public. Without her charge to us, this volume might not have come to be.

Biographies of the contributors are listed alphabetically in a separate section at the end. You will find in them not only a sketch of the committed and serious efforts of each author in the arena of interreligious relations, but a sense of the variety and purposefulness of interreligious dialogue and collaboration that continually go on.

Lastly, I offer two caveats and a final word of thanks. The first caveat is this. Responsible interreligious dialogue requires paying attention to several questions. As many of the chapters in this volume explore, these questions include who is included, what is intended, and what are the actual fruits or effect of the dialogue. Without attention to such questions, interreligious dialogue can become the privilege of the select few or, worse, a tool in the dynamics of political power.

Second, it is important to acknowledge that we are not in this volume presenting a set of interreligious voices. The decision to present only voices from within the NCC family was governed by both practicalities and humility. Practically, it would have been far too large an undertaking to try to collect multiple voices from each of the five interreligious dialogues that make up the NCC currently and from each member of the IRR Convening Table. Nor does this volume represent the true scope or full import of these dialogues, since each of the five are mutually hosted and "branded" by the other five religious bodies as well as the NCC. The volume was launched when Tony Kireopoulos—our friend, collaborator, and leader—was still serving as Associate General Secretary of the NCC and in that capacity as Director of Interreligious Relations and Collaboration.

The initial shaping of this volume was one of Tony's parting gifts. He has now retired from his work with the NCC, leaving behind a legacy of both institutional leadership and deep friendships across religions and around the world. He is a man who walks the talk, and we dedicate this volume to him.

E. E. Thompson

PART 1

Growth and Healing Through Interreligious Relationships

1

Walking Humbly: My Journey of Interreligious Engagement

Kah-Jin Jeffrey Kuan

Discovering God Beyond the Boundaries

I was born and raised in Malaysia, a country once hailed as a grand experiment in multiethnicity, multiculturalism, and multireligiosity. Ours was a world where mosques, temples, and churches stood within walking distance of one another. Their bells, gongs, and calls to prayer wove together the daily rhythm of life.

Yet, despite this rich diversity, the Christianity in which I was raised was deeply evangelical and exclusivist. The conviction that salvation was found "through Christ alone" was not merely theological—it was existential. We were taught that people outside the Christian faith were lost, and our calling was to "save" them. I grew up with what I would later call a kind of religious arrogance, dismissive of other faiths and unable to see the divine in them.

My mother was a Christian, but my father's side of the family was Buddhist and steeped in Chinese religiosity. Family gatherings were often marked by an unspoken tension between these two worlds. As a teenager, I thought of my faith as something that divided rather than united. I remember moments when prayers for my paternal relatives were tinged with pity or even fear—fear that they were somehow outside the reach of God's grace.

Then came a moment that began to unravel that narrow vision. While I was studying theology in college, preparing for pastoral ministry, my paternal grandmother passed away. She had never "accepted Jesus as her personal Savior." When the news came, I was overwhelmed by a sense of failure. I felt I had failed to "save" her soul. My theological framework crumbled beneath me. I was plunged into a crisis of faith: What kind of God would condemn a loving grandmother simply because she had not prayed a particular prayer?

In my confusion, I turned to one of my professors, a United Methodist missionary. With deep patience, he helped me see that my concept of God had been far too small—that I had, in effect, put God in a box. "You cannot play God," he told me. "Let God be God." That simple truth cracked open a door in my understanding. I began to realize that the mystery of God could never be fully comprehended or contained within any one theology or religious system. If God truly is infinite, then God must also be free—free to reveal divine love in ways beyond my imagination, beyond the boundaries of my own faith. That moment marked the beginning of my journey toward pluralism.

Learning from Ah Ma

Around the same time, I began dating the woman who would become my wife. Her maternal grandmother—whom I affectionately called *Ah Ma*—was a deeply spiritual woman, a practitioner of Buddhism and Chinese shamanistic traditions. She served as a healer and counselor in her community, someone to whom neighbors turned for comfort, ritual, and wisdom. Even though she knew that I was studying to be a Christian pastor, she never once criticized my faith.

Our conversations were my first real interreligious dialogues. Sitting in her living room or around her dining table, we talked about compassion, goodness, and peace. I was struck by her calm presence and her sense of moral responsibility toward others. Her faith was not abstract—it was embodied in care for the people around her. From her, I learned that religiosity was not defined by doctrine alone, but by a way of being in the world.

In Ah Ma's gentle way, she became one of my earliest teachers in interreligious engagement. I learned more about Buddhism and Chinese religiosity from her than from any seminary textbook. Her spirituality, though expressed differently from mine, revealed to me another facet of divine reality. She taught me that religious dialogue is not about debate or persuasion—it is about encounter, listening, and reverence for the sacred in another person's life.

Becoming a Christian Pluralist

Years later, as my own theological understanding matured, the lessons I had learned from Ah Ma continued to shape how I understood my vocation as a theologian. In 1991, I was invited to the Pacific School of Religion to interview for a faculty position in Hebrew Bible. During the interview, Professor Durwood Foster, a distinguished theologian, asked me, "How would you define yourself theologically?"

I paused, and almost without thinking, replied, "I would define myself as a Christian pluralist." It was the first time I had ever used that term to describe myself. I explained that I understood pluralism as the conviction that the truth claims within other religious traditions are equally valid, and that Christianity is but one of the many paths through which human beings encounter the divine. Yet, I added, to be a true pluralist, one must also be deeply rooted in one's own tradition. For me, that meant grounding myself within Christianity while remaining open to the truth and wisdom that God reveals through others.

To my surprise, Professor Foster later told me that my answer had earned his vote of support. Over the years, he would occasionally refer to himself as a Christian pluralist, always giving credit to me. What had begun as a spontaneous response became, over time, a defining description of my theological identity.

Living in a Religiously Plural World

My personal journey toward pluralism unfolded alongside the broader transformation of the societies I lived and worked in. In Malaysia, multireligiosity was simply a fact of life. In the United States, where I have spent most of my professional life, religious diversity has likewise become increasingly visible. The demographic shifts are undeniable: the once-dominant Protestant population has declined, while those identifying with other faiths—or none—have risen steadily.

Religious diversity is not a future we await; it is the present reality in which we live. The question, then, is how we engage it faithfully. Interracial and interreligious marriages are now common.[1] Our neighborhoods and workplaces are mosaics of belief and culture. The challenge is not how to avoid diversity but how to engage it faithfully.

Diana Eck, in her germinal work on pluralism, reminds us that diversity is merely a fact, but pluralism is an achievement. Pluralism is not just the passive coexistence of differences, nor is it mere tolerance. It is the *active engagement* with diversity, the seeking of understanding across lines of difference. It involves dialogue—listening as well as speaking—and the encounter of commitments, not their erasure.[2]

That distinction has been crucial in my life and ministry. Pluralism does not mean abandoning my Christian faith or blurring its particularities. It means bringing my commitments to the table and being willing to learn from others who bring theirs. True dialogue is not about agreement; it is about relationship.

Deepening the Theological Ground

My understanding of pluralism was further shaped by the work of Wesley Ariarajah, a friend and colleague, whose book *Your God, My God, Our God* helped me see that religious pluralism has evolved in several directions.[3] Early pluralists sought to affirm all religions as equally valid paths to the same ultimate reality. Later voices, including Ariarajah himself, urged humility—acknowledging that we cannot fully know or judge the spiritual paths of others from within our own limited experience. In its more mature form, pluralism recognizes that religions may not be saying the same thing at all; they may have distinct, even contradictory understandings of ultimate reality. Yet plurality itself is something to affirm, for it reflects the diversity of human experience and the freedom of God's self-disclosure.

As a biblical scholar, I have found that Scripture itself invites us into a more generous theological imagination. In the Book of Micah, we find a vision of a religiously plural world that is at once startling and hopeful:

> For all the peoples walk,
>   each in the name of its god,
> but we will walk in the name of the LORD our God
>   forever and ever. (Micah 4:5)

Micah's words have long resonated with me, especially as I've sought to understand what faithfulness looks like in a multireligious world. In Micah's eschatological vision, nations stream to the mountain of the Lord, yet they retain their distinct identities. There is no demonizing of other deities, no compulsion toward uniformity. Instead, peace and harmony are grounded in mutual respect and the pursuit of justice. Micah dares to imagine a world in which faithfulness to one's own God coexists with respect for others' paths.

That prophetic imagination challenges the exclusivism of my youth. It reminds me that humility—not arrogance—is the mark of true faith. To "walk humbly with your God" (Micah 6:8) is to recognize that our understanding of the divine is always partial, always in need of the corrective of love, justice, and compassion.

Lessons from Asian Theologians

My engagement with Asian theologians has further deepened this conviction. Asian theologians have long wrestled with how to affirm both the uniqueness of Christ and the multiplicity of divine manifestations. My former colleague C. S. Song, for example, urged Asian Christians to see God's redemptive activity beyond the boundaries of Western missionary Christianity. He argued that just as God acted in Israel's history, so too God acts redemptively in Asia's histories—through the struggles and sufferings of its peoples.[4]

Similarly, my friend and fellow biblical scholar Archie Lee explored the intersections between Chinese and biblical creation stories. In the ancient Chinese myth, the goddess Nu Kua shapes human beings from yellow earth. Unlike Genesis, where God breathes divine breath into humanity, the Chinese narrative lacks a divine-human distinction; it even includes a social hierarchy embedded within creation. Yet both myths, in their own ways, express humanity's search for meaning and origin. When placed in dialogue, they reveal both resonance and tension.[5]

These comparative reflections remind me that dialogue does not require synthesis. Indeed, collapsing differences can be dangerous. The goal is not to make all religions say the same thing, but to let each speak its truth clearly, even when those truths stand in creative tension.

Coming Full Circle

Years later, I would find myself co-convening the Buddhist-Christian dialogues of the National Council of Churches. It was a full-circle moment—a return to the interreligious conversations that began with Ah Ma, but now in an institutional and theological context. In those gatherings, I saw again what I had first experienced in her living room: genuine curiosity, mutual respect, and the recognition of the sacred in the other.

These dialogues are not easy. They require patience, humility, and courage. Yet they are essential to our witness in a pluralistic world. They remind us that faith is not a fortress to be defended but a bridge to be crossed. Each encounter with someone of another tradition becomes an opportunity to discover anew the boundless creativity of God.

A Grandfather's Funeral

Even as these dialogues unfolded in academic and ecclesial contexts, the most profound tests of pluralism remained deeply personal. My journey toward interreligious maturity found its most personal test in 1982, when my paternal grandfather passed away. He had been a devout Buddhist and a kind, gentle man. As the second oldest grandson, I was expected to take part in the funeral rites. By then, I was already a pastor. Many in my family and church community disapproved of my participation, fearing that it would compromise my Christian faith.

Yet deep in my heart, I knew that this was something I needed to do—not out of theological confusion, but out of love and respect. My parents understood why I needed to do it, and their quiet support gave me strength. Alongside my cousin, I helped carry the symbolic paper carriage meant to bear my grandfather to the other side. It was an act of filial piety, a gesture of love that crossed the boundary of belief.

Participating in those rites did not weaken my faith; it deepened it. It reminded me that honoring another's faith does not diminish one's own. Rather, it affirms the mysterious breadth of God's grace. In walking the path of religious pluralism, I have not lost my Christian identity—I have found it renewed and expanded, grounded more deeply in humility and compassion.

Walking Humbly

Looking back, I realize that my journey of interreligious engagement has been, above all, a journey of unlearning. I had to unlearn the fear that difference is a threat, the arrogance that assumes God speaks only my language, the impulse to control divine mystery.

Today, I understand pluralism not as a theory but as a way of discipleship—a way of walking humbly with God in a world of many faiths. It calls me to live with openness, to listen deeply, and to trust that God is at work in ways I may never fully comprehend.

The world of Micah's vision still feels far away: a world where nations beat swords into plowshares, and people sit unafraid under their own vines and fig trees. Yet I believe that vision begins in the small, daily acts of dialogue, in the courage to honor another's truth without surrendering one's own.

Ah Ma taught me that. My grandfather reminded me of it. And the God who is beyond all our knowing continues to draw us—Christians, Buddhists, Jains, Muslims, Hindus, and all peoples—into *the divine mystery of compassion and peace.*

2

Friendship at the Heart of Interfaith Relations

Kathryn Mary Lohre

Partnerships and Friendships

Over the past twenty-five years, there have been several critical inflection points in interfaith relations: the terror attacks of September 11, 2001; the massacre at Oak Greek Gurdwara on August 5, 2012; the murderous attacks of October 7, 2023; and subsequent war and genocide in Gaza, to name a few.

Researchers have pointed to the 9/11 terror attacks as the catalyst for a stronger, more robust interfaith movement in the US and globally.[1] Building up interfaith partnerships has become common knowledge as a best practice for responding to community and social tragedy and terror. (The same is true with regard to effective, proactive interfaith engagement, as well.)

Partnerships serve an important purpose. They are the formal, established relationships between representatives and their organizations that foster mutual understanding and support cooperation for the common good. They support the common ground between people and communities without denying the real differences that exist. They are often the professional bridges between organizations and initiatives. Partnerships are indispensable to interfaith relations. They are *life-giving* for the people and communities involved.

But partnerships are one thing. In each of the inflection points I named above, and more, it was not my interfaith partners who first came to mind, though they did—it was my *friends* of other religions or worldviews most directly impacted. The mere thought of how they might feel was disturbing to me, turning my own response toward empathy with theirs. Because of my deep care and even love for them—amid the specific contours of their lives—their burdens weighed heavily on my heart.

Friendships are spaces of intimacy where space is held for sharing identities, core convictions, fears, hopes, misunderstandings, and longings. They bind together our mutual commitments to seeking harmony and navigating discord. Friendships require us to be more vulnerable, elastic, trusting, and forgiving. The fondness we experience for our friends captures our hearts and imaginations, allowing us to see and defend our differences as more gray areas of distinction than black-and-white divisions. Authentic friendships override our "official" roles and demand our real lives. As a result, they are *life-shaping* for the people involved.

This has been my experience.

Interfaith Friendships

I know better than to generalize my own experience into a thesis. At the same time, friendships defy objectivity. Their very subjectivity is what shapes our experiences and attitudes in indescribable ways. Friendships that cross over religious identities have the potential to shape interfaith relations in ways that are not necessarily academic. In the minutiae of our friendships, we are able to see new possibilities for connection that open us more fully to ourselves and our shared humanity. Thus, I will risk being anecdotal for the sake of illustration.

During the COVID-19 pandemic, my oldest son was completing an asynchronous unit titled, "Five Ways September 11 Changed America." The questions included: "What is the War on Terror?" and "Infer why anti-Muslim violence grew." For a child born seven years after the fact, it was a history assignment. As I reviewed the curriculum, my heart found its way back in time to my lived experience of September 11, 2001, the first day of my middler year at Harvard Divinity School.

On that beautiful, sunny morning I walked to Divinity Hall for registration. I was excited for my courses to get underway and was relishing the ease of the first days of the new academic year. One of my closest friends was returning that morning from New York to Boston, and we intended to meet up that afternoon—a rare, unfettered afternoon. But first things first.

As I stood in the registration line with my peers, excitedly discussing our summer experiences, a member of the staff hurriedly wheeled over a media cart and turned on the television. Everything came to a standstill as we watched the attacks on the Twin Towers and the Pentagon unfold in real time. Almost immediately, the pundits began speculating about Islamic terrorists. As a student of religious pluralism, I immediately knew how dangerous this discourse was—that it would lead to acts of anti-Muslim discrimination, hatred, and violence directed at innocent people. I could feel my panic rising for my friend on the flight: a Muslim American.

Over time, we had become close through the typical ways we get to know our friends: stories, conversations, and shared experiences. I knew a bit about what it meant to him to be Muslim—the strength of certain beliefs and practices, and dissonance with others. I had heard his opinions on Israel/Palestine, and his concern for how those tensions played out in his home community, in our country, and globally. In certain ways, he made it clear that growing up a brown kid of first-generation immigrant parents had been difficult, at times. I had experienced his most defining characteristics time and again: his kindness and decency toward others, including strangers, and his genuine curiosity and openness to all.

This is the person I was thinking about when I repeatedly tried his phone number, wondering where he was, or even if he was still alive. All I heard was a busy signal. The phone lines were jammed, and the airports had all been shut down. In fear, my worry turned to anger. Within hours, the public discourse had already become unapologetically anti-Muslim. Anyone perceived to be Muslim was no longer safe. For me, it wasn't a generalized narrative. It was personal. How could anyone hate my friend simply because of his background and beliefs? How could I protect and defend my friend, and by extension, his family and community?

In the days and weeks that followed, these questions were front and center for me in my work at the Pluralism Project, a research project on the changing religious landscape of the United States.[2] Through the lens of my own interfaith friendship, I had experienced the humanity of American Muslims, and I wanted to find effective ways to convey and invite people into that experience. It sounds simplistic, maybe even trite, but there is power in a single friendship to shape our positive regard for an entire community, and our impulse to counteract any threat directed at them. I wondered if it was possible to harness this power.

I was relieved when my friend's number came up on my phone a few days later. It turns out his plane had been diverted to Canada, where he and his fellow passengers were welcomed and cared for by the local people. While other passengers banded together to rent a car to drive across the border, he stayed put. He wasn't sure if it was safe for him to re-enter the US. After about a week, he found his way back to Boston. He didn't say so, but I know he was afraid. As a White, Christian woman, I struggled to relate to his experience, but I had no problem relating to his emotions. As his friend, I could feel his anguish, his anxiety, his anger, and as his friend, I wanted to carry some of that burden with for and with him.

9/11 was a defining moment, for individuals and communities in the US and around the world who experienced unthinkable fear, loss, trauma, and grief. For many—including brown, Black, and Asian people in the US, especially those perceived to be Muslim—9/11 was also a moment of being *re-defined* yet again by the White supremacist narrative of the dominant culture as less than, other, or guilty by association. (One of the first hate crimes after 9/11 was the murder of Balbir Singh Sodhi, a Sikh man in Mesa, Arizona, who was presumed to be Muslim.) My friend's story was but one of millions.

So was mine. As I continued my research at the Pluralism Project, with the questions I held close to my heart, I discovered that my experience was not mine alone. I read a news story about Betsy Wiggins, a Christian woman from Syracuse, New York, who felt compelled to do her part. In the days after the attacks, she called the local Islamic Center, asking what she could do to help the women of the *masjid* (mosque). She was introduced to Danya Wellmon, one of the women leaders. Betsy invited Danya to her home for coffee, which was the beginning of a beautiful transformation. Through friendship, a small movement of mutual understanding, respect, and solidarity grew.

They, too, wanted to share their life-shaping experience. They expanded their effort by inviting their friends to join them. Two weeks later, twenty women gathered at Betsy's home. Eventually, the group became known as "Women Transcending Boundaries" (WTB), which flourished for more than fifteen years.[3] On the basis of their friendships, the women of WTB engaged in spiritual exploration, service, and storytelling.

I found other examples too. I began to see how friendship *is itself* a form of strong and healthy interfaith relations. In different configurations, Muslim, Buddhist, Jewish, and Christian women were building bridges of understanding and solidarity on the basis of their friendships. WTB was one of more than a dozen "Women's Interfaith Initiatives After 9/11" that I helped the Pluralism Project to convene at Radcliffe in 2007.[4] In our research, we categorized efforts like WTB under the interfaith typology of "relationship-building."[5] In this typology, fostering friendships serves as both the means and the ends to deeply transformative interfaith work.

My own experience was validated, in a sense. I began to see more broadly what is possible in the liminal spaces of our deeply held, personal relationships. Addressing suffering, breaking down assumptions, tending to misunderstandings, or coming to know that which is previously unknown holds real power for the individuals, their families, and their communities. By engaging with others through friendship, we also come to know ourselves, to befriend ourselves. Friendship is a form of interfaith that focuses first and foremost on our common humanity, as a precursor to the common good addressed most effectively through partnerships. Interfaith friendships shape our lives so that, together, we can change lives for the better.

Partnering with Friendship

My goal, in the end, is not to create a false binary between interfaith partnerships and interfaith friendships. Both have their particular value and purpose: to be life-changing and life-shaping, respectively. The point is not to abandon partnerships in favor of friendships. Doing so would only diminish our capacity as interfaith practitioners to affect the common good for all people and the planet.

Yet, partnerships alone are insufficient. We cannot affect the common good if we do not know each other deeply enough to know what that actually is. I would posit that one solution is to infuse our interfaith partnerships with authentic friendships. While this sounds simple, or even redundant, it is quite demanding. An interfaith partnership infused with authentic friendship demands something more of us—something more vulnerable, more personal.

Almost every interfaith practitioner can tell you that the heart of interfaith work is the relationships. But what do we actually mean? Interfaith work is no longer simply a movement, but a professionalized sector—with staff, budgets, and strategic plans. These are all good things, but in a professionalized space, "relationships" often refer to the person-to-person interfacing that is guarded by organizational missions and programmatic designs. Understood in this paradigm, the heart of interfaith work is the partnerships [relationships].

Infusing interfaith partnerships with authentic friendships requires us to prioritize personalization over professionalization. It also means allowing for the strength of friendships beyond official interfaith efforts to guide our impulses to uphold our common humanity and care for creation. Perhaps what is most difficult is that, in the end, it requires allowing ourselves to be changed in relationship to one another as friends so that we might be the change.

This is messy, complicated relational work that sometimes leaves more questions than answers. But it is real. It is powerful, and it can be harnessed. In my experience, and also in my research, I believe that partnering with friendship is truly where the interfaith movement is. The question is whether or not we're courageous enough, as people who have strong affinities to interfaith initiative and organizations, to actually move with it, as friends who partner.

Conclusion

In the twenty-five years since September 11, 2001, we have seen the impact of those who responded to the tragedy that began to unfold that day with acts of solidarity. The exponential growth of the interfaith movement over a quarter-century should encourage us in our convictions that our common humanity is stronger than any act of terror, hatred, or violence.

Alongside the first responders who rushed into the chaos of the burning buildings, there were other first responders who rushed into the smoking rubble of the false narrative of "us" vs. "them" to build bridges of "we." It has been my experience that interfaith friendships are the most durable and enduring bridges of "we."

In a time of piercing polarization, we have the opportunity to strengthen the interfaith movement by infusing our interfaith partnerships with interfaith friendships. In so doing, we will strengthen our capacity for life-changing acts of transformative justice, shaped by our lives as friends, traveling together on a common journey of empathy, compassion, and peace.

When the next inflection point occurs, who will you think of first?

3

The Gifts of Difference: Learning to Pray

Margaret R. Rose

Since its founding, the National Council of Churches has recognized that interreligious engagement has a crucial connection to the more specifically ecumenical (Christian denominational) work of church unity. The most recent update of its policy statement, "Interreligious Relations with a Focus on Peace" (2019), is an affirmation of the 1999 statement which recognized "the growing importance of nurturing relationships with communities of other faiths as central to the work of building Christian unity and [integral to] our efforts for peace and human development."[1]

Many NCC member churches have similar documents, outlining their own principles and offering guidelines for denominational and ecumenical interreligious work. The Episcopal Church, for example, in 2023, approved its updated policy called *Holding Difference Together*,[2] a sequel to the 2009 statement *Toward Our Mutual Flourishing*.[3] These are just two of the documents that underscore the theological urgency of this work in a multireligious world, to say nothing of the need for bridge building amid increasing religious polarization at home (in the US) and abroad. Religious literacy, peace building, love of neighbor, and more all provide the groundwork for deeper study and action among people of faith as well as creating tools for addressing larger social and religious divisions.

This reflection, however, is not about sharing information on religious literacy or even about ways religious traditions have so much in common or can serve the goal of Christian Unity. In fact, quite the contrary. It is not, I believe, in the quest for sameness that dialogue is most effective, not in our similarities or even what we have in common, but rather in paying attention to the gifts of our differences. It is about who we become when listening for and opening ourselves and our communities to those differences, not just out of respect, though that is vital, but because in so doing, we deepen our own self-knowledge, and I would venture to say, deepen the faithful and authentic practice of our own traditions.

This reflection is a personal one, about my own transformation and healing, that was only possible in a deep and often vulnerable sharing with one whose faith and practice are very different from my own. As my Lutheran colleagues say so well in their book, *Engaging Others, Knowing Ourselves*,[4] that is the experience I offer in this essay.

It was April 2013, Boston, Monday, Patriot's Day. And since 1897, also Boston Marathon Day. On sabbatical from my church-wide job as Ecumenical and Interreligious Relations Director of the Episcopal Church, I was grateful to spend a semester as a Visiting Fellow at Episcopal Divinity School in Cambridge, Massachusetts. Regular worship included a weekly Eucharist on Mondays at noon and, as it happened, I was the preacher that particular day. The text (coincidentally or not!) was from Hebrews, "Let us run with perseverance, the race that is set before us" (Hebrews 12:1). Glad to preach, I was disappointed that I would miss watching my runner niece cross the marathon finish line, just across the river on Boylston Street. Tracking her progress via internet, I knew she was on target for a personal best.

That is, until the news of the bomb.

Thankfully, my niece finished the race just before the explosion but along with others was caught in the mayhem and the smoke. Too many were not so lucky. We now know that five were killed and almost 300 injured as a result.

Thus began a days' long lockdown and search for the perpetrators. Eventually they were found: one brother who died in the chase, the other arrested and still incarcerated. Both were young immigrants whose family moved to the US some years before. Raised in the Muslim tradition, they attended local Cambridge schools, and with their parents had been granted asylum in the US.

Prayers on all fronts and religious traditions were offered: for the injured, for those who died, for the traumatized, and for the two who were so quickly presumed guilty. Candlelight vigils included those of every faith and none. The public yearning, it seemed clear, was for some way forward that did not add to the polarizing world already evident, even in 2013.

By the end of the week, the lockdown was over. The wheels were in place for ensuring that "justice would be done." Already, though, I was not alone in wondering at the meaning of such a phrase. What is justice in light of what could never be undone: decisions made, lives lost, bodies broken, trauma never to be forgotten.

The tragedies of those days were not lacking in anti-Muslim tropes, stereotypes, false accusations, fearmongering and increased violence against those deemed to be complicit. In sharp contrast, there were many solidarity witnesses for peace, care for the injured and even for the families of the brothers. The week that followed was filled with many images: giant posters and markers put up in public places for people to share their grief and sadness. "Boston Together, Boston Strong" was the mantra along with interfaith gatherings and forums addressing what were thought to be "the issues": *Religion and Terror* was the title of one panel from Harvard Divinity and The Kennedy School.

Mass shootings in public spaces were not yet so commonplace as in recent years, in spite of the 9/11 events. But the shock of this bombing in 2013 became all too quickly part of a dawning realization that an era of increasing violence was upon us. No amount of wishing, or prayer, or even action could relieve, reconcile, or ignore.

My own confusion offered no words or explanation, except a yearning to be in touch with some wider vision and future that would heal these deepening fissures, and a desire to pray. But for what? How? And with whom? It would be easier to yield to anger, to blame and pretend to understand a motive, to be afraid, condemn, and simply numb oneself (myself) in the gratitude that my own loved one was spared. Yet none of those was the answer to the pervasive and ill-defined anguish that filled the air of Boston and its surroundings.

By Friday I found myself heading to church, specifically to St. Paul's Episcopal Cathedral on Boston Common, where I knew there was a Eucharist at noon. And shortly thereafter Jummah prayers, in the undercroft (assembly hall below the church).

For almost 30 years, the Cathedral has offered its space to Muslims for Friday prayers. It is primarily visited by those who worked in the city and whose home mosques were too far away to travel on Friday noon. The Cathedral was a place of welcome, living true to its own mission as "A House of Prayer for All People" (Isaiah 56:1-8). In its recent renovation, the Cathedral now shares its main sanctuary for Friday prayers and built a footbath in its undercroft.[5] As part of the ecumenical and interreligious work of The Episcopal Church, I'd visited and met in mosques and even prayed there. The stance of the Shoulder to Shoulder Campaign—a multi-faith coalition founded in 2010 to counter anti-Muslim attitudes and actions—was familiar, as an expression of solidarity among those who pray, a way to ensure the prayers of all reached to the heavens.

And I'd been to this Cathedral many times, as my first call after ordination. But this day on this occasion was different. I came, equipped with scarf—yet to a worship space and way of praying I did not know. Graciously welcomed, I entered the women's space, carved out of an upstairs room overlooking the main hall. The women—twelve of us—were in the small space above, peeking over the balcony rail to see the four hundred men below. When the women knelt to pray, I sat on the bench at the rear, reverently I hoped, not wanting to intrude, and listened to the sermon.

But as the prayers began again, one of the women approached, took my arm and without a word showed me where to stand, just so, right next to her, foot to foot, shoulder to shoulder. She touched my knee indicating how to kneel and place my head on the floor in prayer. She was a gift of some Holy Spirit, filling the room and my own soul. My silent prayer was, "Lord, teach me to pray." In those moments there was no doubt for me our prayers were ascending to the God who created us all and that both of us were yearning for peace.

As the service ended, the Cathedral dean, standing with the imam, spoke a word of welcome. He named the sadness of the time, noting that he'd just come from the prayers of the Eucharist in the chapel upstairs, and then continued, "I believe God is rejoicing right now, that you are here. We are, in our different ways, somehow praying together. It has been a violent week and we stand [in] solidarity and [as] one asking God to help us work for peace together. Thank you for coming to pray here in this cathedral. Thank you for the blessing that you are to us and for our future together." As the small group of women and the crowd of men left the Cathedral that day, I was not the only one with tears. And for me, prayer itself had become not only a full body experience but also one in which my soul was renewed. Engaging the other, that day gave hope for the days to come—that at least the relationships here could be mended. And not because of our sameness but the gifts of difference. In that moment this Muslim woman of prayer and her practice of it was the greatest gift to my own. It did not erase the commitment and identity to Christian witness, but strengthened it.

The heart of interreligious dialogue is precisely this. As we offer insights, practices, gifts, and our own shortcomings, we know ourselves more deeply and grow in appreciation of the religious diversity of the communities in which we live. Moving away from sameness as we work toward a coming future offers tools for building bridges we might not once have imagined.[6]

Such an experience, where "the other" is the one of who shows the way to faith or healing or wholeness, is grounded in biblical tradition. The story of Naaman, a mighty warrior and the king's commander, who suffered leprosy and was cured by paying attention to a servant girl's instruction (2 Kings 5:1-14); the story of Ruth, a Moabite woman whose act of faith in returning to Israel becomes part of the genealogy of Jesus (Ruth 4:2-18); Jesus' well-known parable of the good Samaritan (Luke 10:25-37); the Syrophoenician woman (Mark 7:24-29); the woman at the well (John 4:5-30). These are only a few of the texts that tell the unexpected story that the one outside our own circle may well hold the answer, indeed the gift, we most need to receive.

Such stories and parables from Scripture are certainly not always like this. There is war and carnage and religious violence in those ancient times and throughout history—and no guarantee of peace or reconciliation. But in such experiences, there is a moment, if only that, of understanding, of relationship with a stranger who becomes a neighbor, and hope is reborn.

These texts, among many others, along with personal life-stories are an invitation to move beyond what we know, to live into respect for every human being, and to receive the gift of diverse humanity and religious many-ness that completes our own.

Knowing the need of the other and others, having the courage to engage with difference, to say yes to those beyond our kin, builds bridges and communities of resistance and are, I believe, the engagements that heal a broken world.

4

Interreligious Work Can Heal

Edward E. Thompson

This chapter was previously imagined as part of an introduction to the anthology, in part to give a foretaste of the kind of stories to be found in later chapters. I share the following story here, simple as it is, to show the power of interreligious engagement for healing at the personal level: in unexpected ways and specifically as religious persons. Personal healing is not the ultimate aim of interreligious efforts; there are loftier goals and achievements, as other contributions describe. However, there is the possibility—the divine possibility—of healing through interreligious work for the individuals involved as well as all the good desired for society more generally.

I say "possibility" rather than "promise" because there is no guarantee that any given relationship will make oneself more whole, nor can one be promised that interreligious endeavors will always go smoothly. To the contrary, when going well interreligious engagement leads to the deepening of human relationship in which there is almost the certainty of uncomfortable moments. But I have come to believe, in part through interreligious engagement, that what is truly healing for the self is intertwined with what is truly healing of the whole. So perhaps it can be said that those engaged in interreligious work can look for personal growth or healing as signs that their efforts—our efforts—have us on the right path. It does matter how uncomfortable moments and other difficulties along the way are handled, a point that leads to the second part of this chapter.

The Story

Before seriously engaging in interreligious work, I would have brief encounters with people of other traditions that left me puzzled. Two stand out, in which I was left with the impression that my conversation partners truly did not understand Christianity. More disturbing was the feeling of a certain loaded quality to their comments, a kind of challenge to my faith. Why did they feel compelled to say such things? But in those early days, in seminary and as a young priest, I lacked the skills and the compelling sense of possibility that I would have needed to take those conversations further. It is, of course, impossible to follow up on every stray comment or misunderstanding, but I wish for those moments back again. In the following story, I am in the hands of someone with the skills and heart for the healing power of interreligious relationship and collaboration.

After several years in parish ministry, I took a leave of absence to enter graduate studies in conflict resolution and peacemaking, with a focus on religions. By then, my wife and I had a son, and I had a new parent's magnified anxiety for what the next generation would inherit. This was a few years after the terrorist attacks in the United States on September 11, 2001. There was a lot of interreligious strife and bigotry, and I came to feel an urgency for the church to do more to be part of the solution of violence in the name of God. What did it signify, for instance, that the Rwandan Genocide occurred, according to the organization African Rights, when Rwanda was "the most Christian nation in Africa"?[1] I had much to learn.

As part of my studies at George Mason University's School for Peace and Conflict Resolution, I joined a field practicum in "citizen diplomacy"[2] in Syria. Organized through the University's Center for World Religions, Diplomacy and Conflict Resolution, the practicum was co-led as a dual-narrative study trip by rabbi and professor Marc Gopin and Aziz Abu Sarah, a Palestinian peace activist and author. Tensions were high in Syria. This was in 2010, one year before the beginning of the civil war, and there were very few Jews left in the country. We knew that there were governmental eyes on us and the various civil groups with whom we met. I do not think I realized at the time what these conditions were doing in me.

Soon after our group arrived, Professor Gopin gave a seminar in Damascus prior to our going out in the field. I offered a comment, he replied, and I thought I had offended him. I was mortified and wrote him a note about it. He invited me to dinner, and over dinner I broke down: "The idea that I, a Christian pastor, would have offended you, my Jewish professor . . ." Had I given him to feel I thought I was superior? I was in tears over the weight of the Christian history of persecution and indifference toward the well-being of Jewish people, particularly in Europe, where he had lost family in the Holocaust. He responded, simply and gently, "I know, I know." It was as if he received what was on my heart. Then he said, "Eat your soup." I followed his guidance, recovered my composure, and thus began a formative relationship. Some years later, Marc would invite me over to his house to share in conversation under the tent of Sukkot, the Jewish festival in remembrance of their ancestors' years of journeying in the Sinai wilderness. Indeed, in some way we were on a journey together.

To the extent our religions have given us to think we should be enemies of one another or have nothing to gain from one another, we need one another across religions to learn and put into practice a better way. Even one hour of interreligious engagement can take on lifelong meaning, nor should we dismiss the courage even one hour takes. On that same trip to Syria, our study group met with the imam of Damascus, who said (as I remember his words), "We are all by blood part of the same human family." The day after our meeting, which was televised, the imam received death threats.

As the story suggests, it does matter how moments of interreligious exchange are handled. Some moments will be completely unscripted, in which case one must bring to bear whatever spiritual resources, knowledge, and training one can. Other interreligious moments can be shaped in advance. In the following section, I offer a few methods for shaping interreligious exchange, drawing in part from peace and conflict studies. Some of them show up in other chapters in this volume, and the list is only illustrative, not comprehensive. Still, they may be useful to suggest something of the variety of approaches that can be fruitful in interreligious relations.

Approaches to Interreligious Dialogue and Collaboration

Before describing a few more formal methods, a word should be said about working alongside one another in serving the needs of others. That itself should be considered an approach. Many religions, certainly all three of the Abrahamic religions (Judaism, Christianity, and Islam), emphasize the imperative to serve those in need, including those outside of our natural circles of relationship. Working side by side can help people bypass what may be differences in religious belief that could be impediments to deeper relationship. Bigotry is often the unintended consequence of never having had positive interaction with people different from ourselves, and working side by side emphasizes our common humanity in the circle of giving and receiving. The organic storytelling about family and the practicalities of life that can occur while working together in caring for others is a powerful force to break down prejudice. That said, until one can talk about the deeper things, a relationship can only go so far. For religious people, this means talking about their religious commitments and practices as part of the totality of their lives. And to the degree there are obstacles to mutual respect and understanding because of religious difference, ways of working through those obstacles become at least helpful, and perhaps necessary. Following are a few approaches that work for interreligious dialogue and collaboration, some of which are elaborated on in other contributions.

Scriptural Reasoning is a method that began as an effort to bring Jews and Muslims together in shared study and contemplation of sacred texts. Later, Christians joined in this method, and it is now practiced by adherents of many religions in countries around the world.[3] While the method is philosophically grounded, the practical basis of it is to allow the members of a particular religion to serve as the experts in the room when reading a text together. Members of other traditions are encouraged to ask questions. The experience of the "experts" in the room is often to encounter their own sacred text with fresh eyes. The presence of someone with facilitation skills is helpful, and training in the specific method is available. In my experience, it seems to work best when there is someone in the circle with a degree of knowledge about the text in question. It also helps, though it is not required, for there to be a good matching of personal experience with reading texts across the religious traditions. If only one religion has a scholar of sacred text in the room, it can become a teaching session rather than a mutual exploration. But the method absolutely does not require the presence of religious scholars, which is part of its beauty.

The Pluralism Project, founded and directed by Harvard professor Diana Eck and already becoming known among religious leadership, offers an approach for interreligious exploration that deserves wide use.[4] The methodology takes a case-study approach to engage curiosity and sharing across religious lines.[5] Participants are given a real-life dilemma in an interreligious setting and are invited to share how they would respond to the situation, then given information about how the actual people in the situation did respond. The richness of the method is in the discussion centered on why people thought and acted as they did. This approach can be used with members of a particular religion or in an interreligious setting. Again, facilitation skills are needed, but there are now many case studies from which to draw. The Pluralism Project website is more generally an excellent place to explore for a broader introduction to religious pluralism in America and constructive ways of living into that pluralism.

Travelling together is another pathway rich with possibilities for interreligious exchange, when undertaken in the right framework. A method I still favor is the dual-narrative approach such as I experienced with Marc Gopin and Aziz Abu-Sarah. People who study narratives, and particularly narratives in conflict situations, attest to the grip "conflict stories" have on our imaginations.[6] As in the familiar adage, hearing both sides of the story fills in the gaps which otherwise allow us to disparage and even dehumanize those with whom we are in conflict. Many years hence, I well remember the power of the dual narrative given on tour by Marc and Aziz in Israel. The people leading the tour must be of a mindset to welcome the voice of the other for interreligious repair to occur.[7]

Lastly, I will name the Insight approach as fruitful for interreligious engagement. The Insight approach puts participants in touch with the basic patterns of human questioning and deciding. It was first given formal shape from philosophical analysis of successful interpersonal conflict resolution in a therapeutic setting.[8] It was then developed more broadly as an approach to group conflict, notably to help police develop self-awareness in order to avoid unnecessarily aggressive action.[9] The approach opens up to self-awareness and mutual exploration processes of valuing as well as how we come to think what is factually true. Therefore, there is ample room in the approach for spiritual seeking of ultimate values and wisdom from sacred texts.[10] It can be used in interreligious settings to open up areas of conflict for mutual exploration, and it could fruitfully be used in any interreligious collaboration where people want to unpack their thought processes and decision-making. Using the Insight approach well takes a solid introduction and some practice.

These are just a few formal methods and approaches for interreligious engagement. There are many ways people have found to engage across religious boundaries, as a simple online search will reveal and other chapters in this anthology describe. Meeting an acquaintance of another religion for lunch, particularly when both are open to discussing how religion shapes their lives, is a type of interreligious engagement. The few methods and approaches described above are meant to underscore that if you are interested in interreligious dialogue and collaboration but do not know how to begin, or if you have gotten stuck somewhere along the way, there are ample resources to help you. As in most things, the quality of preparation and leadership matters; but the most important thing is to begin.

Conclusion

According to Jesus' summary of Judaic law and prophetic teachings, loving our neighbors is a primary way of loving God more deeply (Matthew 22:36-40). In a world of religious pluralism, loving our neighbors means coming to know and love our interreligious neighbors. The wisdom of the Greatest Commandment (loving God) and "the one like it" (loving our neighbor) resonates in the wisdom of other religious traditions, as the imam's words made clear to me in Damascus many years ago. There is always the divine possibility of what in Judaism is called *tikkun olam,* healing the world, and deeper relationship with just one interreligious neighbor can lead to so much more. Loving neighbors across religions is also a way of coming to love ourselves more deeply. As Jesus makes clear in the same passage from Matthew's Gospel, we are to love our neighbors as we love ourselves (Matthew 22:39). When we share in deeper knowledge and love with our neighbor across interreligious boundaries, we are involved in God's work—in the world and in each of us.

PART 2

Gifts and Challenges of Interreligious Engagement

5

"There's a Wideness in God's Mercy": My Engagement with Islam

Clinton Bennett

First Encounters

My Christian engagement with Islam began in September 1978, when I became a missionary candidate at the Selly Oak Colleges, Birmingham, designated to work in Bangladesh. A recurring theme in my subsequent engagement with Islam has been the realization that much of what we believe theologically may be true but is not exhaustive of truth, which leaves room for paradox on such issues as whether God is One, or One in Three Persons, and on how essential explicit faith in Jesus is for salvation. I like Anselm's definition of theology as "faith seeking understanding," which suggests that our attempt at understanding faith continues throughout life and, who knows, perhaps beyond![1] While apparently irreconcilable theological differences stand between Christians and

Muslims, I am persuaded that our speaking about God is fallible, that God is more than either of our theologies think, and that there is a "wideness in God's mercy" and to God's love that surpasses our understanding.[2]

Exploring religions such as Hinduism and Buddhism as an undergraduate at the University of Manchester (1975 to 1978), while also training for ministry at the Northern Baptist College, I found a great deal to challenge and even deepen my faith. My upbringing had depicted these religions as spiritually bankrupt, but as I studied them it became increasingly difficult for me to dismiss them as totally futile, false, or misguided. This led me to question some of the assumptions of my upbringing about the relation between God, religions, and their followers. On July 2, 1978, persuaded that missionary service was my vocation at least at that stage in my life, I was ordained and set away for work in Bangladesh, although I had not yet read a single book on Islam, and Bangladesh is a Muslim-majority country. At Selly Oak, I enrolled in the certificate in the study of Islam under David Kerr (1945–2008), director of the Center for the Study of Islam and Christian-Muslim Relations. At CSIC, Professor Syed Hasan Askari (1932–2008), the first Muslim faculty member at a Christian institution, and David, were hugely influential on my thinking, as was Lesslie Newbigin (1909–1998) who taught missiology. His *The Gospel in a Pluralist Society* (1989), which rests mission with God's Spirit, greatly challenged my thinking.[3] My upbringing as a Baptist in Australia was conservative evangelical, but by the time I offered for missionary work my thinking had changed. I became convinced that the church's mission includes working for social justice, the elimination of poverty, and community solidarity against political oppression and economic exploitation, as well as preaching a message of individual salvation. I believe that God wants us to enjoy health and wholeness in this life, not only to secure a place in paradise after death. The "social gospel," pioneered by the Baptist theologian Walter Rauschenbusch (1861–1918) and the more recent proponents of liberation theology, influenced my thinking.

David Kerr set out to teach us Qur'ānic Arabic and the foundations of Muslim faith and practice without intruding his personal opinions into the lectures, so that we encountered Islam, as nearly as possible, from a Muslim perspective. Hasan Askari was happy for David to teach these courses because he trusted that David would not distort what he taught with Christian polemic or criticism of Muslim beliefs. Hasan preferred to lead class discussions on spirituality more generally. He also taught a Bible study on John's Gospel. Hasan espoused a spiritual humanism that looks beyond labels and external rites to inner experience of the sacred at the human level. Experiencing how David could teach about Islam without showing hostility, and how Hasan could expound the Bible with reverence and deepen my understanding of the text, raised questions that I had to consider. In one of many references to Jesus' Sermon on the Mount, Hasan invites Muslims and Christians to read this together, "to read together the Sermon on the Mount, both for Christians and Muslims, is to bear witness to one of the deepest inter-religious involvements known to history."[4] Reading together leads to the realization that "Jesus, like all prophets, is contemporary to all times."[5] For Hasan, the sermon is about "unity and love" and ethical solidarity.[6] David taught us to recite portions of the Qur'ān without ever impugning what we read and obviously had a love for and appreciation of the book as if God's word could indeed be heard speaking to us through this non-Christian scripture. He did nothing to detract from the beauty of the Arabic. Many earlier Christians had derided the Qur'ān as repetitive, absurd, clumsy, confused, and contradictory, lacking any appealing qualities even if only literary. We also visited mosques where we observed Muslim prayer and attended seminars with students and staff at the Islamic Foundation, Leicester. I began to treat with profound suspicion the claim by some Christians, including many Baptists, that God does not respond to or hear Muslim or Jewish prayer.

Could people for whom Jesus is not the Second Person of a Trinity truly know God, who for Christians exists in a Trinity? I began to doubt that I had the right to judge anyone else's relationship with God or lack of one. I saw Hasan Askari, and other Muslims whom I met, as godly women and men whose prayers and acts of devotion were offered sincerely, whose lives arguably displayed all the virtues that I hope others see in mine which I claim to be a Christ-centered life. This questioning meant that, when I went to Bangladesh, I was much less confident that my task was to "win souls" for Christ. When I reached Bangladesh, what I began was more of an open-ended experience of encountering Muslims, listening and learning from them, than a one-way communication of light into darkness, or of truth against falsehood.

Yet the insistent question that kept me occupied was this: Does such an openness somehow betray my Christian faith? The two authors whose writings have most assisted my thinking here are Lewis Bevan Jones (1880–1960), a fellow Baptist, and Kenneth Cragg (1913–2012). My first trip across the border from Bangladesh to India in 1980 was to attend the fiftieth anniversary celebration of the Henry Martyn Institute of Islamic Studies, Hyderabad, which Jones had co-founded.

Since then, I have lectured and carried out research there during several visits. Jones pointed out that, while we may say that God's "self-revelation in Jesus Christ, is in every way adequate to human need . . . we . . . cannot claim that God is, in Jesus, exclusively revealed."[7]

Cragg's *The Call of the Minaret* (1956) opened new possibilities in Christian-Muslim encounters. Less concerned with doctrinal disputation, Cragg sees the mutual exploration of spirituality and devotion as areas where Muslims and Christians can find affinity. For Cragg, conceptual convergence is more important than literal or verbal congruence between the two faiths, speaking of what he called "inter-theology." In *The Pen and the Faith* (1985), Cragg commented that Askari's "reading of the Qur'an suggests lively possibilities of Muslim-Christian kinship and, so doing, central areas of interior questioning for both."[8] I believe that a faith that fails to constantly ask questions about itself is complacent and lifeless. Might I discern real faith in Muslim lives and hearts? Despite his deep recognition of Muslim piety at the personal level, Cragg attracted criticism for addressing an allegedly abstract Islam that will one day metamorphose into Christianity toward which it has always pointed. Years later, I was able to meet Cragg when he spoke at a conference I organized while working at the British Council of Churches.

Bangladesh: My Journey Continues

I reached Bangladesh in October 1979. My first year was spent in full-time language study at the Oriental Institute in Barisal. I was subsequently based in Khulna, then in Rangpur. I taught theology by extension for the Bangladesh College of Christian Theology and pastored a local congregation in both cities. The Muslims whom I met in Bangladesh were very different from the hot-headed fanatics I would see in Western media representations after 9/11. They were generous, tolerant, community oriented, deeply spiritual men and women who were in the main inclined to support a secular democratic Bangladesh. Despite my relatively short time in Bangladesh, this was a life-changing experience.

Return to Birmingham

Returning to Birmingham, I completed my MA (1985) and PhD (1990) at the Center for the Study of Islam and Christian-Muslim Relations. The Birmingham Ethnic Education and Advisory Service (BEAS), set up by P. C. Chakravarti, MBE, recruited me for my Bengali speaking ability. Working mainly with the Bangladeshi diaspora, we encouraged neighborhood self-help and educational programs. The task was to contact people in the community—door-to-door visits were involved—and invite them to meetings to discuss forming self-help neighborhood associations and the type of activities they would like organized. I helped mosques with planning permissions, charitable registration, and funding for educational activities. Some saw this work as a betrayal of the gospel that required me to confront Muslims with their errors not to facilitate their religious practices; but for me this was being a good neighbor. A lot of my work took me into local schools, and I was soon co-opted as a governor by one of the schools where we worked. I was active within the local ecumenical council, the Interfaith Council, and from 1985 as associate pastor of Highgate Baptist Church. Our neighbor was the Birmingham Central Mosque where one of the Trustees was a close friend. We organized exchanges with us visiting them and them us.

At the British Council of Churches

In August 1987, I was appointed executive officer of the Committee for Relations with People of Other Faiths (known as CRPOF) in the Mission Division of the Council. My committee chair (moderator), the Right Reverend Jim Thompson (1936–2003), then bishop of Stepney, was also co-chair of the Interfaith Network for the UK. My post at the BCC involved attending the committees of those member communions that had established interfaith advisory bodies and serving on the executive committees of the Council of Christians and Jews, the World Congress of Faiths, and the newly established Interfaith Network. Through the Interfaith Network (founded 1987), I developed a close relationship with Dr. Zaki Badawi, Hon. KBE (1922–2006), former imam of the London Central Mosque and founder of the Muslim College, Ealing. Zaki and I issued joint press statements during my time at BCC, responding to the Rushdie affair and the Gulf War of 1990–1991. Zaki defended Rushdie's freedom of speech, arguing that Muslims who found the book offensive should write a critique, or ignore it, not try to kill him. We both thought that diplomacy had not been exhausted before use of military force began in Iraq. Many British Muslims found themselves at odds with public opinion in the UK on these and other issues.

I also took part in various World Council of Churches dialogue meetings including two, both in Switzerland, as part of the drafting team for *Issues in Christian-Muslim Relations: Ecumenical Consideration* (1991). This experience helped develop my understanding of the dynamics and aims of interfaith dialogue. I regard myself as a practitioner of dialogue as described in the WCC's Guidelines (1979) but especially as redacted by CRPOF into four principles first published, with commentary, in 1981. These are:

1. Dialogue begins when people meet each other.
2. Dialogue depends on mutual trust and mutual understanding.
3. Dialogue makes it possible to share in service to the community.
4. Dialogue becomes the medium of authentic witness.

Much of my work at CRPOF involved encouraging member churches to adopt these at synods, conventions, assemblies, or conferences, and producing a new explanatory publication, *In Good Faith* (1991).

After the BCC

In 1992, I joined Westminster College, Oxford, as a lecturer in the study of religions (later senior lecturer), resident tutor, and assistant chaplain, remaining there until 1998. While at Westminster, I represented the Baptist Union on the World Council of Churches' Consultation on the Church and the Jewish People, attending meetings in Geneva and Budapest. After Westminster, I was an associate professor of religion, specializing in Islam at Baylor University, Texas, between 1998 and 2001 followed by a period working at a community school in Birmingham where over 95 percent of students were Muslim. From 2008 until 2024, I taught religious and Asian studies at the State University of New York at New Paltz. I acquired US citizenship in 2012. In 2012, I became a Recognized Clergyperson of the Alliance of Baptists, a small Baptist denomination whose stated principles and commitments align with my own. The Alliance is committed to social justice, equity, collegiality, and diversity. It ratified a statement on Muslim-Christian relations, the first by a Baptist body, in 2003, that apologized for how Baptists have done little to adjust a theology that "nurtures an attitude of cultural supremacy . . . over" Muslims or to "counter the prejudice of centuries."[9]

Since 2012, I have participated in the *Christian-Muslim Relations: A Bibliographical History* project based at Birmingham University. Team members include leading Christian and Muslim scholars of Islam, through dialogue meetings co-sponsored by the NCC and the United States Council of Muslim Organizations since 2014. I have become convinced that, beyond theological discussion, cooperation on matters of common social concern calls us to build bridges, break barriers, and prioritize love of God and of neighbor rather than engage in endless debate. Our meetings have taken place in mosques, churches, a seminary, and a denominational headquarters.

A Wideness in God's Mercy

The fourth CRPOF principle states that dialogue becomes a medium of authentic witness, which means that we can share our deepest faith convictions and spiritual experiences with our partners, whose response might be to embrace Christianity just as ours might be to embrace their religious faith. Dialogue enables faith sharing in ways that are more likely to attract a positive response from hearers than expressions of hostility toward the faith they love and cherish.

Accuracy in what we say about Islam is equally important, thus avoiding bearing false witness. Faith sharing works best when we ground this in our personal experience, rather than insist on exact doctrinal formulations. On Trinity, I have argued (drawing on Jones), that we can speak about how our experience of the divine is expressed through Trinitarian language, rather than dogmatize on the absolute need to subscribe to the Nicene Creed. Perhaps we need to think of our theological ideas as wholly true about God and the divine-human relationship, yet not the whole truth, leaving room to learn from others' theologies. Unless we think that we are God's equal, there should be room for mystery, even paradox and ambiguity. Some of our differences may confound and perplex us, yet this we know: God's spirit moves within us. Even while recognizing apparently unresolvable stumbling blocks such as whether Jesus did or did not die on the cross, collaborating with Muslims in making the world peaceful, just, equitable, and sustainable—as Qur'ān 5:48 encourages—might end up pleasing God more than theological controversy.

6

Interfaith Challenges in Ministry

Whitney Bodman

How does one teach a religion that is not one's own? And why?

This is a question that constantly challenged me as I moved from pastoring a church to teaching Comparative Religion at Austin Presbyterian Theological Seminary. I needed to justify the seminary requirement that all MDiv students take a course in comparative religion. This argument had already been made in the early '80s when the seminary decided to establish a position in World Religions. I was the second person to fill this role. I still had to justify the requirement to every new class of students. This I could do with anecdotes from my own pastoral experience.

The anecdotes indicate the practical reasons for learning about other religious traditions. They are not the main reason. The German sociologist, Max Müller, once said that to know one religion is to know none. One understands most everything by contrast. *This* is not *that*, and understanding the difference between the two expands the understanding of each. In the stories below, beyond fulfilling my pastoral duties, I come to understand something about Christian theology and practice by seeing it in contrast to the practices of Hinduism and Judaism.

The Death of a Hindu Child

How do you do a funeral as a Congregational pastor for a thirteen-year-old girl tragically killed by a car while walking to school? Her father was Hindu, and her mother, a Mormon. I was an interim pastor at the Original Congregational Church in the small town of Wrentham, Massachusetts, a town of about 10,000.

The funeral of a schoolchild is a community event. Her schoolmates would be there, and teachers, other parents, and of course, extended family. The service could not be simply the Congregational Free Church ritual that I would conduct for a member of my congregation. This service involved children who had lost one of their own. And it involved an interfaith component that had to be addressed. The challenge was to offer sensitivity and respect to those who mourn—Hindu, Christian, and other—while maintaining the integrity of one's own faith and ministry.

I had a passing awareness of Hindu concepts of death and funeral practices, but I consulted several Hindu colleagues who also had interfaith experience. I needed to understand, at a minimum, what words, rituals, and symbols I could include in the ceremony that would be meaningful to the Hindus and acceptable in a Christian service. My investigation was far more than what was required for this service, but I am interested in such things, so I went beyond the call of duty, so to speak.

Everything in Hinduism is governed by *Dharma*, which could be understood as the Law of the Universe, the design of reality, the interrelationship of all things. As part of *Dharma*, our journey through life and beyond it to new life is governed by *karma*, the law of cause and effect. Everything has a cause and every cause has an effect. The passage of this child's life into a new life through reincarnation would be governed by *karma*. This is not a bad thing. It should not be regarded as a condemnation. It is simply the logic of the interconnectedness of everything.

Hindus believe in reincarnation. The soul, the *atman*, will go through a 10- to 13-day transition to a new body, born as a new person, except in certain exceptional circumstances. That period of transition must be carefully managed since the soul, in that period without a body, is vulnerable. The concept of the soul's vulnerability during periods of life transition—particularly birth, coming of age, and death—is common in many religions and is found in certain periods and places within Christianity as well.

Christians do not believe in reincarnation. We believe that the person, the soul, transitions to heaven, which is a one-time event. Each soul, at conception or birth, is a new creation of God, not a reemergence of a soul from a previous life. At death, each soul, embodied in one way or another, ascends to God (or perhaps is condemned to hell!). Except for the concept of purgatory, these are permanent assignations.

Generally, at Christian funerals, I see a confidence that the person who has died will go to heaven. God's grace and mercy abound. For Hindus, that is less of an issue because there is always a future incarnation in which a soul may benefit from good *karma* with a better life.

For both Hindus and Christians, we are never apart from the loving care of the divine. Death does not interrupt that, even though it deeply disrupts our lives. In that service, however, we understood the nature of the divine—and our understandings are quite diverse, not only among our different religious traditions but within them—we trusted, we knew, that God continued to carry that child with love and care. Though Christians do not believe in reincarnation, we do, like Hindus, believe that death is not the end of existence. As Paul says, death has lost its sting (1 Corinthians15:55-57) because whatever happens after death, we are still in the loving care of God. That fundamental principle is something that Christians and Hindus share, and therefore it was on that idea that I focused in the design of the service.

In the town of Wrentham, we all shared the deep pain of loss. We shared uncertainty as to how to move forward in grief and through grief. God had given us each other to support and sustain one another. It was a time to share not only this child's story, but also our own stories in which she now played a part.

Unfortunately, the passage of time and multiple transitions to new computers and software have resulted in the loss of my notes and the homily for that service. It was nearly 30 years ago. I no longer remember her name, sadly, but I remember sitting with the family and the remarkable sisters who stepped in so strongly not only to participate and guide the service, but to help the school community cope with the tragedy and the grief.

In the service, I read a passage from the Indian poet Rabindranath Tagore that could have been Christian poetry. The two sisters read from a Hindu text, perhaps the Bhagavad Gita. In my homily, I made some brief comments about the candle, placed by the head of the body to help guide the soul along the path to new life. The little that I said about concepts of death and life after death in Christianity and Hinduism was honest and generous about both. Mostly, I talked about grief, the anguish that is common to us all.

The Education of Children in a Mixed Marriage

How do you counsel a Christian woman whose husband is Jewish and whose in-laws are now making demands for the Jewish education of their young grandchildren?

This also occurred as I was the interim pastor in Wrentham. She attended church fairly regularly, but I did not know her well. As she described the situation, her husband was not a practicing Jew. When they were married, they avoided a heavy emphasis on Christianity, but the interfaith dimension of the relationship was not emphasized in the service. I do not know what sort of preparation the pastor did prior to the wedding. It clearly did not adequately address the possibility that religious commitments might play a larger role once children arrive on the scene. That is so often the case that a wise pastor should spend a considerable amount of time exploring not only the feelings of the couple about the upbringing of their children, but also other factors (such as the expectations of parents) that might play into that conversation.

My responsibilities were twofold. The first was informational. I told her about Jewish sensitivities about intermarriage and the continuation of the tradition. The contemporary Jewish writer, Emil Fackenheim, dramatized this as "granting Hitler a posthumous victory" by letting the Jewish people gradually waste away. He asserted that the continuity of the Jewish people was the 614th commandment. (In Jewish tradition, there are 613 commandments in the Torah.) For her in-laws, the Jewishness of their grandchildren was far more important than the Jewishness, or lack thereof, of their son's wife. It represented the survival of the tradition.

Christians tend to think about Judaism solely in terms of a religious tradition. It is more than that. There is a strong sense of peoplehood apart from religion. Jews are not simply those who practice the religion of Judaism. Neither is it accurate to describe them as an ethnicity. The best terminology may be peoplehood. One need not practice the religion of Judaism to be, and consider oneself to be, a Jew. The husband's parents were not only concerned about the religious education of the children. They were also concerned that the children understand themselves to be a part of the Jewish people.

Losing that sense of membership in the Jewish community would also mean that they would gradually become part of the Gentile community that often looks upon Jews with hostility—anti-Semitism. Hostility to Jews has such a long history that Jews are always aware of the potential of danger, even to the point of elimination. Nothing clarifies this more than the Holocaust. All of this danger lurked in the background of the concern for the education of the grandchildren.

The second task was pastoral. What was she going to do with this information? A part of the issue was certainly her husband's failure to be decisive. She wanted the children raised in her Christian tradition. Her faith was important to her. They had not talked specifically about this before they got married, a failure on the part of the pastor who prepared them. At that time, his Jewish tradition did not seem particularly important to him, and her Christian commitment did not seem to bother his parents. This concern about the children came as a surprise. Her husband seemed unwilling to deal forthrightly with his parents' concerns.

Should they let the children decide, exposing them to both traditions? Is that responsible parenting or simply evading a decision? How did she feel about the children being raised Jewish? How did she understand Judaism? Was Judaism, for her, a rejection of Jesus Christ? For that matter, how did her husband understand Christianity?

We did not have the opportunity to follow through on the process of thinking through the decisions that needed to be made. My interim pastorate ended. I do not know what the couple decided.

I sympathize deeply with the concern of Jews for the future of their tradition and their people. I see how often the Jewish tradition is wrongly understood in Christian Bible study and preaching. Much of what I was taught in seminary decades ago about the Jewish tradition in the New Testament was wrong.

Given that the Jewish Scriptures—the Old Testament in our terminology—is Scripture for us, and the New Testament is infused with Jewish tradition, we cannot understand our faith accurately without understanding some aspects of the Jewish tradition. We are religious siblings.

Furthermore, given the long history of hostile relationships between Jews and Christians, I believe it is also incumbent upon us to develop positive and supportive relationships with our Jewish neighbors. This is even more true given the volatility in the Holy Land. We are all struggling with the violence, the rights and wrongs among Israelis and Palestinians. Listening and speaking, primarily the former, are part of our call to peacemaking.

A Parade of Questions

These are two stories from my pastoral experience, but the parade of questions has been never-ending.

I have conducted many interfaith weddings, each one different. Some require working with clergy from another tradition who will have their own requirements and peccadillos. A Jewish groom asked that I not mention the name of Jesus during the ceremony out of concern for his grandmother, a Holocaust survivor. I talked a lot about God.

How about ceremonies for people who have affiliations with more than one tradition? Will you let them include readings from the Hindu Ṛg Veda, the Navajo Blessing Way, or the Buddhist Heart Sutra? Is it okay for them to stomp on a glass—a Jewish tradition—or have an image of the Hindu Lord Ganesh on an altar in front?

How do you respond to a local synagogue that requests to use the sanctuary of your church for High Holy Day services? Is it okay if they cover or remove Christian symbolism? Is this a measure of Christian hospitality or is it a violation of consecrated space? Our church hosted a local synagogue first for the High Holidays, and then, as they grew, for weekly Shabbat (Sabbath) services. The movable crosses were set aside, but no attempt was made to cover the discreet cross on the screen in front of the organ pipes. We saw this as encouraging a community with whom we had done much work in the town community.

What about the immigrant Somali Muslims who work in the meat-packing plant? The people in the community, even in your congregation, are understandably worried that they are terrorists, a danger to the community. They speak another language, dress differently, and do not readily associate with non-Muslims. What are the avenues—and goals—of outreach to them and counseling the larger community? What do you need to know, and how will you become rightly informed? A former student wrestled with these questions in a small town in Colorado.

Would you include pagans in the local ministerial organization? When a woman opened a shop in town selling crystals and literature on rituals associated with witchcraft, she wanted to come to the Ministerial Association to talk about what she was doing. Two of the members objected strongly.

Ministers often get questions about various organizations identified as cults. Frequently, it is because a family member has become involved, or the organization has moved into the neighborhood. Is it safe? Is it demonic? Is it brainwashing? It is important that a pastor be a source of good information, not repeating popular rumors or the propaganda of cult deprogramming organizations, some of which are themselves not unlike the cults they oppose.

In an increasingly diverse nation, we have a population often given to experimenting with practices and wisdom from an endless variety of sources, some associated with established religious traditions, and some from, well, wherever.

Studying other religions is preparation for ministry. In fact, it is preparation for simply living in this nation and loving the neighbor who is burning sage in her backyard or fasting during the Muslim month of Ramadan.

7

Some Benefits of Interreligious Dialogue

Darrell Jodock

I grew up in a rural community in North Dakota. My family and I were active in a church, but none of us had any contact with anyone who practiced another religion. When I was in my 30s, initial interreligious conversations had the flavor of an adventure—an enjoyable and challenging and enriching adventure. Such conversations have not threatened my Christian faith. Yes, certain ways of understanding that faith have been challenged in ways I could not have anticipated, but even this experience has been valuable.

My first interreligious experiences started with Jews in 1978, and I have stayed involved in Jewish-Christian dialogue ever since. Conversations with Muslims and others came a little later and have been more sporadic.

To my delight, the Jewish community and the Muslim community have, from the beginning, been wonderfully hospitable—not only to me but also to my students when they would attend services. They would often report that they had been welcomed and that someone from the congregation had explained what was happening and answered their questions when it was over. To cite another kind of example, when my then-twelve-year-old son needed blood, the first person to give was a member of the local Jewish community.

Understanding Christianity Better

There are, I think, at least three benefits of interreligious dialogue. The first is that it helps Christians understand Christianity better. In about 1990, the Institute for Jewish-Christian Understanding in Allentown, Pennsylvania, which I had helped start, organized some living-room dialogues. In each case, members from a local church and members from a local synagogue met together regularly for conversation, without any clergy or religion professors present. A one-page introduction identified the topic for the evening and offered conversation-starting questions. The guidelines started with religious events and experiences and then moved into differences in teachings. The conversations seemed to go well, but after three or four sessions, participants were asking for help understanding and explaining their *own* religion! In response, we organized evening sessions during which a Christian teacher and a Jewish teacher each explained their tradition's understanding of a common theme, such as the nature of God or the role of religious community or the like. Prompting a person to learn more about basic teachings and to understand them more deeply is one benefit of interreligious dialogue. But there are others.

A Christian who has grown up with "I believe" statements can sometimes not consider how they came to be and what they entail for relationships with God and other humans. Trying to explain them to those in another religion can prompt a person to understand how self-involving, relational, and tinged with mystery those claims are.

Interreligious dialogue raises important questions about the character of Christian teachings. Why do Christians believe what they do? How important is this belief for Christians and Christianity? What are its implications for one's life?

For me, specific changes have arisen from within interreligious dialogue—issues Jews and Christians have needed to address together. One has to do with God's relationship with massive human suffering and with the Holocaust as a specific case study. Probing the issue together has been helpful and even in some ways necessary in order to avoid any implication that Jews somehow deserved their suffering. If a person (Jew or Christian) were to say that God is in control of all that is, so that God either causes everything to happen or specifically allows some things to happen, then God would be responsible for the Holocaust. But if God is a God of love and mercy, then that's not possible. Therefore, some rethinking of God's role has been required—for Jews, yes, but also for Christians. In my opinion, the only option with any promise is the view that, in a costly move, God has granted humans freedom and pledged Godself to live with their choices rather than overriding them. The result is that, right along with humans, God suffers the consequences of any human misuse of freedom, while also working with them to end the suffering.

An interesting by-product of this view is that God does not know the future. Yes, because God knows everything that has happened and is happening, God knows more about the future than we do; but if humans are free, then some things

God cannot know until they happen. All of this challenges traditional conceptions of God's omniscience that include knowing the future and the traditional understanding of God's all-controlling omnipotence.

In addition to prompting Christians to rethink their beliefs, interreligious dialogue can also prompt them to rethink their understanding of the shape of religion. That is, in an initial endeavor to understand another religion, the tendency is for Christians to select topics to investigate that parallel their own. For example, beliefs are important in Christianity, so what are the teachings of the other religion? Commandments are important for Christians, so what behaviors does their religion reject? Religious leaders are important for Christians, so what role do their religious leaders play? Up to a point, all of this can be helpful, but it can also bypass those aspects of another religion for which there is no parallel in Christianity. Significant and extended interpersonal contact can widen and enrich a person's understanding of the many components of religious identity. One can discover that the other person values practices and priorities that have no corollary in the Christian's experience. This discovery can lead to a new appreciation of the scope and complexity of religion. And this, in turn, can also enhance one's appreciation of the scope and complexity of one's own religious identity.

Cooperation

This brings us to a second benefit of interreligious dialogue. For me, interreligious dialogue has reinforced the view that religion—and more specifically Christianity—is best understood as a way of life shaped by a sense of mystery, gratitude, and connectedness, along with a vision of what could be.

What could be is that humans love their neighbors—neighbors of all sorts. What could be is that the hungry are fed and the homeless find housing. What could be is that humans work for a healthy planet. What could be is that swords are beaten into plowshares, and spears into pruning hooks, and no one learns war anymore.

The concept of vocation—that is, a calling to serve the neighbor and the wider community—has become ecumenically significant. Members of congregations of various denominations have benefited from workshops and working groups and personal reflection regarding their callings. But it is also a shared priority. Explorations by leaders of other religions have concluded that, though the word *vocation* is not used in their own traditions, the concept is present.[1] This consensus provides a common ground on which to build broader, interreligious networks to serve the larger community and to urge it to take steps toward greater justice.

About four years ago, a group of us living in our town of about eleven thousand people started a Good Neighbor Diversity Council. Along with bringing together various ethnic groups (Somali, Native American, African American, Hispanic, Asian, Yankee, German, and Scandinavian), it has also brought together Muslims and Christians in ways that were not true before. The Council cooperates with the public school, the county, the city, the chamber of commerce, a church-related college in town, the Muslim Center, churches, and other community groups. All of this began with open meetings and conversations co-chaired by a Christian and a Muslim. In those meetings, new programs were devised and, as we all worked to implement those programs, we learned to know each other better. Except for a workshop on Islam designed for non-Muslims, religion was seldom the overt topic of discussion, but we all saw how it affected the lives and priorities of others as we tried to bring together the diverse elements of our community.

One kind of interreligious dialogue is "face-to-face"—that is, it is an exploration of the distinctive teachings of two religions, with each "side" explaining those teachings to the other and exploring their overlap or lack thereof. Another kind of religious dialogue is "shoulder-to-shoulder," exploring what diverse individuals or faith communities can do to put into practice a shared vision of an improved neighborhood. Both kinds of dialogue are important, but the latter leads more directly to a wider engagement and, in that (limited) sense, is more valuable. "Shoulder-to-shoulder" dialogue also creates connections that can be important at a time of tragedy or crisis, when the care and concern of others reassures the sufferers that they are not alone.

When dealing with people in public office, an interreligious approach can be helpful, because it is easier for officeholders to respond to an interreligious group than to members of a single religious tradition. The officeholders are less likely to be accused of favoritism, and they can (usually correctly) assume that the group represents a broader, more sociologically diverse, group of citizens.

For decades, there have been voices loosely and rhetorically describing the United States as a Christian nation. In recent years those voices have intensified, urging Congress to declare that the United States is an officially Christian nation. Not only would this violate the first amendment and be harmful to Christianity, it would also threaten the civic "standing" of people of other religions.[2] In dialogue, Christians can learn how deeply frightening this prospect is to our non-Christian neighbors.

In addition to the form of Christian nationalism that wants the US Congress to declare the US a Christian nation, there is another. Its goal is to take control of the seven areas of public life (family, religion, education, media, arts & entertainment, business, and the government). Influencing public policy in support of human dignity, justice, and humanitarian assistance can be an appropriate calling for Christians, but gaining control (or even trying to gain control) of the sectors of society distorts Christianity and violates the rights of others.

Living with Unanswered Questions

A third benefit of interreligious dialogue is that it teaches us to live our lives, practice our religion, and relate to our neighbors while we continue to have unanswered questions. If faith is trust, then we can believe in God without knowing the answer to every question. We can live with tensions and paradoxes. We can disagree with someone of integrity and neither condemn their ideas nor sever the relationship. There is more than one example of an unanswered question in the Bible, but the one that best seems to fit this setting is Paul's discourse in Romans 9–11, where he tries to understand God's plan for those who have remained Jewish (and, he insists in 11:1, not been rejected by God) and those who have come to regard Jesus as the Messiah. At the end of chapter 11, he throws up his hands and ends with a doxology praising the unsearchable and inscrutable ways of God (11:33-36). He did not need to find an answer to his own important question in order to maintain and celebrate his own faith.

Similarly, I have learned from interreligious dialogue not to be too anxious in the face of unanswered questions. And, by analogy, I would like to propose that our contemporary society would be a lot healthier if it could live with unanswered questions regarding some aspects of public policy instead of insisting on one right answer, condemning opponents, and coercing conformity.

What then about rival choices? Take Jewish and Christian views of the Messiah as a case in point. It is not possible to affirm simultaneously the Christian view that Jesus is the Messiah and the Jewish view that he was/is not. But it is possible to explore and understand why Jews believe as they do and why Christian believe as they do. And it is possible to perceive that "Messiah" in the Jewish setting does not mean the same thing as "Messiah" (or "Christ") in a Christian setting. There is a disagreement but not one of direct opposites. Exploring the differences can be valuable.

When it comes to other religions, I, as a Christian, do not feel a need to endorse their beliefs or practices, as if one religion is as true as another. Nor do I feel a need to flatly reject their teachings, as if their views are all wrong. I am content to admit I don't know, to appreciate any way their religious commitments benefit others or benefit the larger community, and to cooperate with them—to respect and work together for their sake and for the well-being of the world. Should any person in another religion inquire about my faith, I am happy to explain it to them, as best I am able, and even to recommend it and then let them decide how to react to it.

If religion is more a way of life than the affirmation of propositions, then it is also true that religious community matters, and its importance should be recognized. To be sure, the role and shape of religious communities vary from one religion to another and from one cultural setting to another; but coming together in community is important for a variety of reasons. It provides support in the face of tragedy and disappointment. By drawing on a diversity of experiences, it expands and deepens our vision of what could be. In America, Christianity tends to be individualized or homogenized. In neither case is the result a vibrant community.

Conclusion

In this short essay, I have by no means exhausted the list of benefits from interreligious dialogue and cooperation, but I have tried to identify three: it can challenge us to understand our own religion more deeply, it can help us understand the scope of a religion's influence in our lives, and it can persuade us that we can believe and practice the faith without answers to every religious question.

8

Life at the Intersection: Interreligious Dialogue, the Convening Table, and the Practice of Faithful Listening

William L. Johnson, III

Life at the Intersection

My participation in the National Council of Churches' convening table on interreligious dialogue has been both a personal pilgrimage and a profoundly rich ecclesial and interfaith encounter. From the outset, what distinguished this experience was not merely the diversity of religious traditions represented, but the depth of engagement made possible through intentional listening shaped by mutual accountability and a shared commitment to the common good. The convening table functioned as a microcosm of the NCC's broader vocation: to nurture unity without erasure and witness without coercion.

To be welcomed at the table—to speak from within my own Christian faith tradition and lived experience, and to be heard with care and respect—was itself a sacred act. This hospitality of listening reflects a central NCC theological conviction: that the Spirit of God is at work wherever faithful people gather in humility, seeking understanding rather than dominance.[1] Such listening is not passive hospitality, but an active theological posture grounded in trust that God speaks amid difference.

At the convening table, I encountered others not as abstractions or ideological placeholders, but as people of faith shaped by history, struggle, hope, and moral responsibility. In that space, my voice mattered—not because it prevailed, but because it was received. This experience reshaped my understanding of interreligious dialogue as a practice of communion without coercion and witness without erasure. Dialogue became less about arriving at agreement and more about cultivating faithfulness in relationships.

Life at the intersection is never neutral. It is the place where personal journeys intersect with communal crises, where inherited traditions meet emerging realities, and where faith communities are compelled to discern their public responsibilities. At this intersection, I found myself personally in transition even as the church, the nation, and global religious communities faced profound disruption marked by religious nationalism, cultural fragmentation, political polarization, and economic instability. These realities do not exist in isolation; they converge in ways that demand theological reflection and moral courage.

It was within this layered moment that I became acutely aware of God's presence—not always through certainty, but often through holy disruption. God spoke through dialogue, whispered through testimony, and warned through the stories we entrusted to one another. These conversations were not incidental; they were revelatory, calling us toward greater faithfulness and deeper solidarity at a time when both are urgently needed.

Dialogue as Sacred Practice

The convening table offered more than conversation; it offered formation. Together, we listened and prayed. We learned and prayed. We lived with one another—and prayed. Dialogue in this context was not ancillary to the church's work; it was an expression of the church's calling for unity, justice, and peace. Within the NCC tradition, dialogue has long been understood as an ecclesial practice shaped by repentance, hope, and trust in God's reconciling work.

Interreligious dialogue, when practiced faithfully, becomes a spiritual discipline. It requires patience, vulnerability, and restraint. It calls participants to resist the impulse to control outcomes and instead trust the Spirit's slow work of transformation. This posture aligns with the NCC's long-standing commitment to dialogue as an expression of Christian humility and public witness rather than as a strategy for dominance or persuasion.[2, 3]

Dialogue also forms participants by exposing them to complexity. It resists reductionism and invites deeper engagement with the lived realities of others. In this sense, dialogue functions as a school of discipleship, training leaders to navigate differences with integrity and grace. Such formation is essential in a world where faith is too often mobilized to divide rather than to heal.

Seeing God in the Other

One of the most profound experiences of the convening table was the recognition of God's presence in the faces of those different from me. I saw God in the eyes of our colleagues from the Sikh community. I saw God in the eyes of our Jewish siblings. I saw God in the eyes of our Muslim, Buddhist, and Hindu friends. These encounters challenged me to reflect more deeply on what it means to confess belief in a God who creates all humanity in divine image.

This recognition did not dilute my Christian convictions; it deepened them. It affirmed the NCC's theological insistence that honoring the dignity of the other is inseparable from fidelity to one's own faith. To encounter the other is not to surrender identity, but to practice it responsibly. Christian witness, when faithful, is marked not by fear of difference but by confidence rooted in love (cf. 1 John 4:18).

In a world shaped by suspicion and exclusion, the convening table became a quiet act of resistance. It affirmed that faithful people can gather across difference without weaponizing belief. Such gathering is itself a testimony to the reconciling work of God, who calls communities beyond fear into relationship.

Listening as Action

Listening emerged as a central form of action within the convening table. In a culture shaped by urgency and polarization, disciplined listening becomes an act of resistance against domination, erasure, and oversimplification. Listening creates space for truth-telling, repentance, and reconciliation—core themes within the NCC's public theology.

Through listening, I encountered the lived realities of other faith traditions not as abstract positions, but as embodied commitments shaped by suffering, hope, and perseverance. This form of engagement allowed discernment to emerge organically, shaped by trust rather than pressure for consensus. Listening became a way of honoring the agency of self-determination and resisting the temptation to speak for others.

Theologically, listening reflects a confidence that God's Spirit continues to speak through the gathered community. It echoes the ecumenical conviction that no single tradition exhausts the fullness of truth, and that humility is essential to faithful witness. In this way, listening itself becomes a moral act with public implications.

Challenges of the Convening Table

Despite its many gifts, the convening table raises important challenges. Chief among them is the question of translation: how does dialogue move beyond the table into the lived contexts of congregations and communities? This challenge has long accompanied ecumenical and interreligious efforts and requires intentional strategies of connection and accountability.

There is a risk that dialogue becomes symbolic rather than transformative if it remains confined to national spaces. The NCC's theological vision calls participants to carry insights gained into local practices of service, advocacy, and accompaniment. Dialogue must eventually take flesh in shared commitments to justice, peace, and the dignity of all people.

Another challenge concerns representation and power. Those gathered at national tables often have access and resources not shared equally across communities. This reality demands humility and responsibility. Participants must ask how their presence and voices relate to those they represent and serve.

Choices Before Us

Dialogue presents choices. Will we build together across differences, or remain isolated while merely informed by one another? Will we risk collaboration, or retreat to the safety of parallel efforts? These choices shape the moral credibility of interreligious engagement.

The convening table invites a choice toward shared responsibility, rooted in trust and sustained by hope. Such responsibility reflects the NCC's commitment to cooperative witness, recognizing that faith communities are bound together by their shared concern for the common good.

From Dialogue to Transformation

For me, the most significant transformation occurred internally. The convening table reshaped my imagination for pastoral and public leadership, informing how I preach, teach, and care. It deepened my attentiveness to language, history, and the power of narrative.

These internal shifts began to shape external practices, opening space for interreligious collaboration grounded in local relationships. Transformation, I learned, is rarely immediate. It unfolds through sustained faithfulness and small acts of courage.

Living Our Faith in Community

We have lived in our faith communities. We have lived for our faith communities. Too often, we have lived around one another without connecting or communing with one another. The NCC's witness calls us to live our faith in community, recognizing that our commitments find their fullest expression in relationship and shared responsibility for the common good. To live faith in community is to acknowledge interdependence and embrace solidarity as a theological virtue.

Formative Moments at the Convening Table

The convening table dialogues left an indelible impression upon my sense of self, my understanding of my own faith tradition, and my insight into how culture and faith interact—and how they may be harnessed for the common good of society. Over the last several years, three moments have stood out as turning points that clarified my vision, deepened my purpose, and renewed my passion for interreligious engagement.

The first formative experience occurred during our convening table gathering in Chicago, where we engaged in sustained dialogue with our Muslim and Christian colleagues. From the outset, I was deeply impressed by the hospitality and candor with which our conversations began. The dialogue possessed an uncommon depth, allowing us to explore a wide range of topics—from personal faith priorities to global politics. We wrestled honestly with the rise of religious nationalism and examined how political decisions made by the United States reverberate not only domestically but across the globe.

Our Muslim colleagues spoke candidly about the ways American foreign policy and political rhetoric affect communities abroad, often with life-altering consequences. These conversations challenged us to engage uncomfortable realities while resisting the temptation toward defensiveness or retreat. Instead, we were invited into an integrated dialogue that held unity and differences together. What emerged was a shared recognition that, even amid distinct faith traditions and theological commitments, we hold more in common than we often assume—especially in our shared concern for human dignity, justice, and peace.

Equally powerful during this gathering were visits to local schools and community institutions, where we witnessed how faith communities had organized themselves not only for survival and security amid present threats, but also around a shared hope for the future. As an African American man leading within a Black church context, this experience was both insightful and encouraging. It affirmed the power of faith-rooted community organizing and the role of collective memory in sustaining resilience.

The second experience that significantly shaped my sense of engagement and purpose took place during our convening table gathering in New York City, centered on Jewish-Christian dialogue. Our visit to Ground Zero created a sacred and sobering context for reflection. There, conversations around liberation, memory, and reparations in the aftermath of the Holocaust took on a particular gravity.

These discussions extended naturally into broader reflections on religious nationalism, particularly in relation to ongoing conflicts in the Middle East and Gaza, and the ways these realities inform political discourse in the West. As we examined the parallels between Christian nationalism in the

United States and other forms of religious nationalism globally, new clarity emerged regarding the moral challenges that lie ahead. These conversations illuminated how faith can be manipulated to justify exclusion and violence, while also reminding us of its potential to ground accountability and reconciliation.

The third impactful moment from the convening table came not through a gathering, but through a text. Susan Neiman's work, *Learning from the Germans*, became a critical conversation partner in my reflection. Neiman explores Germany's decades-long process of confronting the moral catastrophe of Nazi crimes and the intentional work of remembrance, accountability, and atonement that followed.[4] She draws compelling connections between that history and what may be required of the United States as it continues to wrestle with its own legacy of racial injustice.

Her examination of racism, the Civil War, Jim Crow, and their enduring consequences casts new light on our present condition. As an African American leader, I found her analysis particularly resonant. Once again, religious nationalism surfaced as a force shaping public memory and moral imagination—often obstructing the honest reckoning necessary for healing. This text sharpened my awareness of the urgent need for truth-telling and accountability as essential components of faithful public life.

Each of these experiences has remained with me, continuing to inform my understanding of faith, culture, community, and civility at the intersection. Together, they serve as catalysts for transformative insight, reinforcing the conviction that interreligious dialogue is not ancillary to the church's mission, but central to its witness in a fractured world.

Next Steps: Practicing Faithful Engagement Beyond the Table

The future of interreligious dialogue depends on intentional next steps. Dialogue must continue as a spiritual discipline rather than a programmatic obligation. Insights must be translated into local contexts where faith meets lived experience. Participants must commit to ongoing self-examination, recognizing that transformation begins within.

In a time when forces of division threaten the fabric of public life, the convening table offers a counter-witness: faithful people listening for God together. This witness is not peripheral to the church's mission. It is essential.[5]

9

Making Safe Spaces at University for Interreligious Dialogue

Laura Osborne

Interreligious dialogue is highly important today in our globalized society. Diaspora, people displaced for one reason or another, are forever among us. The Reformed Church in America (RCA) has a long history of working with diaspora communities and interreligious relations, specifically in Muslim-Christian relations. Since 1889, the RCA has been on the Arabian Peninsula, specifically in Oman. This mission is crucial to the conversation around interreligious dialogue, particularly within the RCA. The main religion on this peninsula is Islam. So, the RCA has been serving in predominantly Muslim areas for a long time. The history of this mission and the ripple effect are why I am serving in the RCA today. Throughout this essay, I will examine Islam and its tenets, Christian scripture, and select Qur'anic texts, with a primary focus on why Muslim-Christian dialogue is so important. Throughout this essay, I will share information about my ministry context, where I have served for the past seven years, as well as my time on staff at the denominational level with the RCA.

Interreligious dialogue is extremely important in this day and age. Our neighborhoods, schools, and workplaces are changing quickly, and as Christians, we need to know how to have respectful conversations with those from other faith traditions. The passage from the Bible that sticks with me the most is in Matthew 22:36-40:

> "Teacher, which commandment in the law is the greatest?" He said to him, "'You shall love the Lord your God with all your heart, and with all your soul and with all your mind.' This is the greatest and first commandment. And a second is like it: 'You shall love your neighbor as yourself.' On these two commandments hang all the Law and the Prophets."

When I read the second part about loving our neighbor as ourselves, that is the main Scripture I hear when it comes to interreligious dialogue. I want my neighbor of another faith to respect me and my faith, and in turn, I shall respect theirs. I shall respect their beliefs even if they are vastly different from mine. That is true from lawn care to politics, to religion, and to vaccine mandates. I believe we have lost the art of the healthy conversation in many instances.

In many circles, there is the question of sharing the gospel and conversion. Some would say that interreligious dialogue is fine, but there has to be a point where we share the gospel with others and try to have them accept Christ. While I want everyone to know about Jesus, this can be a radical way to push people out of a relationship, and how many faith traditions are seen in a bad light from the mission history? Not all the history of the mission is beautiful; there is hurt and pain along the way. Mission history can be seen in a colonizing way—the missionary comes and shows what the local people need/want, or takes local land. There is also the missionary version, where they come and ask what the locals need/want and purchase land. The latter, thankfully, is more of our tradition in the RCA. The gospel can be shared in both spaces, but I believe that the second way is more effective. The gospel is shared through relationships and hospitality in the second way. Both ways have merit, but for long-lasting change, there needs to be relationships.

In the twenty-first century, there is much to argue about. Interreligious dialogue is not one of those topics to argue about, but a space to learn and grow together. It is about listening and leaning in. It is an amazing opportunity to learn from one another and build relationships. It is not an easy topic to just dive into, but with practice, it can become part of daily life. I believe this starts and ends with hospitality. When we make hospitable spaces, we can create safe spaces for dialogue.

In *The Oxford Handbook of Religious Diversity*, Sallie B. King has a chapter on interreligious dialogue. Her chapter is very helpful and encouraging to hear the history around this subject. She writes, "Interreligious dialogue is an inevitability in the world today as a result of globalization, the process of bringing together all parts of the world into a single system. As a result of this process, people today in many countries live their daily lives in community with people of other religions as neighbors, schoolmates, coworkers, and friends."[1] Interreligious dialogue can be in a formal setting or it can be quite conversational. In both settings, there is merit, and great understanding can happen.

Interreligious dialogue is a somewhat newer concept. According to King, "The 1893 World's Parliament of Religions is generally recognized as the beginning of organized interreligious dialogue. Held in Chicago in conjunction with the World Columbian Exhibition, it was the first time religious leaders were invited to speak for themselves and their religions on a footing of equal respect and dignity. It was also the first effort to produce an inclusive, global gathering of religions. Although it was dominated numerically by Christian presentations, the parliament was a major globalizing moment. Indeed, it was an unprecedented occasion for east to meet west, not as a colony or as part of an empire, but as an equal, in fact, an attractive and impressive equal."[2] The main point here is that there is an equal standing. There isn't a time when each person is trying to convert the other; it is a time of mutual understanding. There doesn't have to be mutual agreement, but a time of faith sharing in a safe space. There are questions and answers, but no stance that one way is better than the other.

There is a very strong mentality in some nations or cultures with an "us vs. them" mentality. In world history, there are many instances and wars based on different beliefs. This has been a rough history throughout the world. Wars, terrorism, hate, violence, and destruction have been a huge part of world history because of religion. Even in the United States of America, this mentality still exists, the "us vs. them," especially in a post-9/11 world. The United States is a country built on immigrants and migration. Much of the building of our country was forced because of colonization, but most of the people who live in the United States have family members who immigrated from another country; along with that can be other faith traditions.

According to King, interreligious dialogue expanded very rapidly after World War II and Vatican II: "One focus of attention in Vatican II was the relation of the Catholic Church to non-Christian religions. The outcome of the councils' deliberations on the subject was a document called *Nostra Aetate* (In Our Time), which announced a radically changed posture in the Catholic Church towards other religions. Following the publication of this document, the Vatican established a standing office for dialogue—the Pontifical Council for Interreligious Dialogue."[3] *Nostra Aetate,*[4] promulgated in 1965 by Vatican II, is a beautifully written statement on how each family community forms a larger community that we all live in.

Interreligious dialogue is important across all religions, not just Christian-Muslim, although they are the two largest religions. Many parts of the world conflict with each other because of religion. Unfortunately, because of this, many people don't see the value in religion and especially in interreligious dialogue. The dialogues can start small. Everything has to start somewhere; that is a main reason why I really appreciate the Al Amana Center in Muscat, Oman. The mission has been there since 1889, as stated previously, and has morphed over the years, but they have had a steady presence of welcome and hospitality to and with the Omani people.

In the resource *Called to Serve, Essays on RCA Global Mission,* John Hubers writes on the Arabian Mission and discusses the history of the mission. Samuel Zwemer is a name that is synonymous with this mission, and Hubers writes, "Zwemer and his missionary compatriots became close friends with their Muslim neighbors, which made it more and more difficult to maintain the stereotypical caricatures either of Muslims as people or the faith that animated their lives."[5] This laid the foundation for the mission that is seen in the present day. Hubers writes, "The door was now open for a more dialogical approach to mission, even though Zwemer did not go as far in that direction as missionaries do today. How far is evidenced in the current work of the Al Amana Center in Oman, which operates in a cooperative relationship with your money and government to bring Muslims and Christians together for dialogue around matters of common concern while still maintaining a faithful gospel witness."[6] This mission is extremely important to the RCA as a whole.

As mentioned before, our neighborhoods, workplaces, and schools are ever changing and we need to learn how to live, work, and play among and with our neighbors of another faith. From the 2020 annual report from the Al Amana Center, this statement is helpful: "We live in a global age in which one act, whether it is political, economic, religious, or cultural, can have a worldwide impact. Our futures are now interconnected, and it will take the cooperation of all segments of society to live in harmony with one another."[7] The statement continues, "Hans Küng, a world-renowned scholar and friend of Oman, has said there will be 'no peace between nations unless there is peace between religions.' This is the reality of the world in which we live and the need to which the Al Amana Centre is responding."[8] The Al Amana Centre has a faithful witness in a Muslim majority country. They bring groups in to see and hear and experience what they are doing. Alongside that, there are trainings and resources that they provide to the greater RCA. This is incredibly helpful to not just the RCA but to the big C Church as a whole.

The history of the Mission on the Arabian Peninsula and the stories and changes over time are how I am in my role today in the RCA. I have been ordained in the RCA for 12 years. For almost seven of those 12 years, I have been a campus minister with International Campus Ministry (ICM) at Western Michigan University (WMU) in Kalamazoo, MI. The ministry at WMU is a ministry of hospitality and welcome. Students come from all over the world to study, and in turn, seek community. We help build community and help bring students together from different religions and backgrounds. Through this ministry I started getting connected with others doing similar work, some through other campus ministries in the United States and Canada. That got me connected with the Salaam project through Resonate Global Missions in the Christian Reformed Church. This project was helping connect Christians and Muslims from the same area for interreligious dialogue and understanding. Through this work, I was invited to go on a women's trip to Oman in February of 2018. I had heard a bit about their work as it was similar to mine. After this trip, I started partnering with the CRC and helped to create a network called Journey into Friendship.

Journey into Friendship is a network for anyone looking to get connected with their neighbor of another faith or for those who are already doing that work. There are monthly network meetings with various topics and an annual consultation, which focuses on different parts of North America. These topics range from Scriptural Reasoning, refugee resettlement, migration issues, courses, networks, etc. Through this network, I was meeting more like-minded folks from the RCA. I learned that there was an Interreligious Task Force that was formed out of the Commission on Christian Unity. Through that task force, there was a position which was created in the RCA that would focus on interreligious work. In the summer of 2019, I was hired to be the new Coordinator for Interreligious Relations. This position helps churches and individuals connect to their neighbors of other faiths. This work includes a lot of interreligious dialogue. This is extremely important to help break down fear, stereotypes, and questions that both religions have.

The focus of this essay is on Muslim/Christian interreligious dialogue because Islam is seen in such a bad light in the United States media at times. Islam is a religion that has adherents all over the world. I believe this is why it is very important to engage in interreligious dialogue with our Muslim friends and neighbors. It is the second-largest religion in the world according to Gallup. Islam is one of the three Abrahamic religions, Christianity and Judaism being the other two. These three religions have much in common and vast differences.

Islam is a monotheistic religion among the three Abrahamic religions: Christianity, Judaism, and Islam. In Huston Smith's book, *The World's Religions,* he has a chapter on Islam. In this chapter, he unpacks the history, background, prophets, and practices of the religion. When it comes to comparing Islam to Christianity and Judaism, we hear,

> Judaism was correctly introduced through its Shema—"Hear oh Israel, the Lord our God, the Lord is one"—but its teachings were confined to the people of Israel. Christians, for their part, compromised their monotheism by deifying Christ. Islam honors Jesus as a prophet and accepts his virgin birth: Adam's and Jesus's souls are the only two that God created directly. The Qur'an draws the line at the doctrine of the incarnation and the Trinity, however, seeing these as inventions that blur the divine/human distinction. In the words of the Qur'an: "They say the God of mercy has a begotten son. Now have you ordered a grievous thing . . . it is not proper for God to have 'children' (3:78,19:93)."[9]

Islam is one of the fastest-growing religions, according to Gallup. Islam was born in Mecca, Saudi Arabia. According to Islam, Muhammad was the last and final prophet of Allah. According to Dr. Kim's notes and readings, Muhammad was born in 570 AD. Islam was born as a religion after the Angel Gabriel came to Muhammad while he was meditating outside the city. He started teaching and preaching (as prophets do) on what he had heard and seen. He was met with opposition (as many prophets were) but steadied on and soon all of Arabia had embraced Islam by the time that Muhammed had died in 632 AD, according to Dr. Kim's notes.[10] The holy book of Muslims is the Qur'an, and it has a supporting document in the Hadith. The Qur'an was written by followers soon after the Prophet died. It was written in Arabic, and strong Muslims believe that it should only be read in Arabic. According to the Prophet Muhammad, the Qur'an was dictated directly through the Angel Gabriel to him.

In Islam, there are five pillars that are the basic belief system of Muslims: Shahada, Prayer, Charity, Fasting, and Pilgrimage. "Shahada is declaring allegiance to God."[11] Kim states, "The act of saying the creed is in itself a part of the faith. Muslims are to study the Qur'an and recite the phrase, "There is no god but God, Muhammad is the messenger of God," many times a day.

The second pillar, Prayer, is one of the ones that the non-Muslim world sees and hears about the most. There are five times a day when Muslims are to pray. Muslims use the lunar calendar for the timing of the start of Ramadan, but they use the sun for the timing of daily prayers. The prayers are before sunrise, midday, late afternoon, at sunset, and then one more during the night. Friday prayers are most encouraged to be in-person prayers if the person is well. Men are obligated to go, and women are encouraged. Children can attend, but must not be too noisy. Congregants are to sit shoulder to shoulder and toe to toe if possible. The prayers are done in a prostrate position. There is a sermon and the prayer time at these services. Prayer direction should always be toward Mecca, the holiest spot for Muslims in Saudi Arabia. Muslims may recite their prayers anywhere; they don't have to be in a mosque.

The third pillar is Acts of Charity. Some call this a tithe, a tax, or a charitable gift. This is around 2.5 percent of one's income. The money usually goes to charity to be distributed to the needy and can be given at the mosques. Tithing is what we call it in Christianity, and it is talked about a lot in the church. I wonder how much it is mentioned in the mosques.

The fourth pillar of Islam is Fasting. Fasting is done during the month of Ramadan. This time changes slightly each year because of the lunar calendar. Fasting is done in the ninth month of the lunar calendar from sunrise to sunset. Usually, during this time, Muslims' days get quite shifted as they get up early before sunrise, for a meal, and stay up late for a meal. Some skip that first meal if they stay up all night and then sleep during the day. This is fasting from food, water, cigarettes, and sexual activity. Iftar is the breaking of the fast in the evening, and it is usually done in large groups; and it is a large feast. I have participated in a few Iftars in my experience. People who are sick or weak do not have to fast but are still encouraged to pray and reflect.

The fifth pillar of Islam is Pilgrimage or Journey to Mecca. All Muslims are required to visit Mecca once in their lifetime if financially able to do so. I would think of this as a trip to Israel for Christians and Jerusalem for Jews.

The place of worship for Muslims is the Holy Mosque or Masjid. This means temple of place of worship. I have been in countless mosques from the Grand Mosque in Oman to the Hagia Sophia in Turkey, to small mosques in Israel, Egypt,

Kosovo, Albania, and around the United States. Some are incredibly large (Grand Mosque in Oman) to very humble, like the student mosque here in Kalamazoo, Michigan, near Western Michigan University. All require similar characteristics: Be clean (some hand/feet washing stations outside), be quiet (respectful), take off shoes (sometimes a shoe cubby), and separate areas for men and women to pray.

Besides Christianity, my work encounters more Muslims than any other religious group. All of the Muslims that I get to know over time are beautifully generous people. When I say generous, I mean with their time and hospitality. I have had dinner in many Muslim homes and have had many in my home over the years. I am very honored to be brought into their stories as well. Some are very painful, and all are beautiful. I am continuing to learn and love with them around their faith and life. When people say to me, "Don't they [Muslims] try to convert you?" I say that I have been working with Muslims for seven years, and it has never happened. I have been able to share the gospel with them over time, and I grow deeper in my own faith the more I work with people from other faiths. I believe that everyone in a faith community should make friends with others from another faith community. This makes us better neighbors, and it helps to break down fears of other religions and cultures as well.

Having interreligious dialogue with trusted friends makes a difference. It can take a while to build trust with someone. Our ministry is built on creating a safe place for students of any faith to come and find community. We are not shy about what our beliefs are and who our God is, but we share that in a safe way. Students get to know that this is a community that is welcoming and they share that with others. Many of our students come from countries where religion and culture can have blurred lines. I believe that even though our religions are different, it is a safe place to come and meet friends.

Bibliography

Flannery, Austin (ed.). *Vatican Council II: Nostra Aetate (Declaration on the Relation of the Church to non-Christian Religions*. Collegeville, MN: Liturgical Press, 2014.

Hubers, John. "Arabian Mission–1889," *Called to Serve: Essays on RGA Global Mission*, The Historical Series of the Reformed Church in America, No. 102, edited by Charles E. Van Engen, Jean Van Engen, and Sally Tapley, 53-64. Grand Rapids, MI: Reformed Church Press, 2020.

Hull, Hilary. "Al Amana Centre—Building Trust and Peace in Oman and Beyond," n.d. Website: Al Amana Centre: Building Trust and Peace. Accessed November 19, 2021. http://www.alamanacentre.org.

King, Sallie B. "Chapter 8: Interreligious Dialogue." In *The Oxford Handbook of Religious Diversity*, edited by Chad V. Meister and Sallie B. King. Oxford: Oxford University Press, 2010.

Smith, Huston. *The World's Religions*. New York:HarperOne, 1991.

PART 3

Speaking from Our Traditions About Interreligious Engagement

10

Building Bridges of Hope

Archbishop Elpidophoros of America

In the twenty-first century, particularly in the United States, interfaith dialogue is not merely important, but essential to fostering a society grounded in equality, freedom, and community. At its core, fruitful interfaith relations must be cultivated from a recognition of our common humanity as bearers of the image and likeness of God and consequentially, our calling to love our neighbor. No one articulates the great task and telos of human life better than Saint Maria Skobtsova, lovingly known as Mother Maria of Paris, when she, who lived and was martyred out of love for her neighbor, writes that "however hard I try, I find it impossible to construct anything greater than these three words, 'Love one another'—only to the end, and without exceptions: then all is justified and life is illumined, whereas otherwise it is an abomination and a burden."[1] Saint Maria so beautifully articulates, in a rather succinct and poetic fashion, Christ's call to encounter and see him in all people, no matter their race, ethnicity, or religion, and to "love one another" (John 13:34) just as he loves.

In order to truly embrace Christ's call to love our neighbor and thus foster relations of respect, peace, and reciprocity in pluralistic and religiously diverse communities, we must look to both the inherited wisdom of our faith traditions for guidance as well as our own personal experiences so that our witness of love is set on strong foundations. In reflecting on my own upbringing, I am reminded that no matter the complexity or tension that separates one from fulfilling Christ's call to love our neighbor, this command remains ever simple and essential to our salvation. Being born in Bakirköy, Istanbul, to a Greek father and a Syrian mother, my life has been shaped by the unique experience of being an Orthodox Christian of the Romiosini, living in the land of the Ecumenical Councils and Church Fathers, yet living, in many ways, as a stranger in my homeland. From an early age, I experienced the struggles that accompany the religious and ethnic minorities whose status and rights, the state finds, are not determined by one's membership in the human family, but by one's alienation from the majority. Even in the face of such struggles, my soul, by God's grace, was led to service his church and it is in such service that I have found true freedom and life.

No matter one's religion or background, all people yearn to live in freedom. It is in freedom that one is truly able to know oneself, one's neighbor, and God himself. Even when living in the world, in growing up in a society where some were not politically or socially free, I learned at a young and impressionable age the importance of religious freedom as a principle that ensures the embodied and physical manifestations of faith in our world. Still, as the son of Orthodox Christian parents and a spiritual child of His All-Holiness

Ecumenical Patriarch Bartholomew, I realized that religious freedom is not an end in and of itself, but a state of social existence that safeguards the ability of people of faith to express and proclaim true freedom found in the spiritual life. Without spiritual freedom, without repentance that frees one from the shame and isolation of sin, are we truly free? In witnessing those who cultivate themselves in the spiritual life, who yearn for inner freedom found in God, I came to understand that the fruit of spiritual freedom is peace. It is with such inner peace that we no longer fear our neighbor but embrace all.

It is in this spirit of peace that the Eastern Orthodox Church has promoted respectful and peaceful relations among faith communities for centuries. Having suffered from the trauma of religious intolerance and oppression both in the Old and New World, the Orthodox Church remains resolute in upholding the dignity of all people as bearers of the image and likeness of God and protecting the religious freedom of all. Further, over the centuries, the Orthodox Church, being historically situated at the crossroads of faiths and cultures, has encouraged a posture of dialogue and fellowship among its faithful toward other faith communities. Many of our saints, hierarchs, and laity have engaged in dialogue and fostered relations of mutual respect and solidarity, most notably with communities from the Abrahamic faiths. The Church's disposition to foster peaceful relations with other faith communities is grounded in the self-giving love of Christ. This Christo-centric vision of dialogue with our neighbor is most clearly presented by the Hierarchs of the Holy and Great Council of the Orthodox Church, convened on the island of Crete in 2016, who stated:

> A true Christian, following the example of the crucified Lord, sacrifices himself and does not sacrifice others, and for this reason is the most stringent critic of fundamentalism of whatever provenance. Honest interfaith dialogue contributes to the development of mutual trust and to the promotion of peace and reconciliation. The Church strives to make "the peace from on high" more tangibly felt on earth. True peace is not achieved by force of arms, but only through love that "does not seek its own" (1 Cor 13.5). The oil of faith must be used to soothe and heal the wounds of others, not to rekindle new fires of hatred (*Encyclical*, par. 17).

It is through this vision of dialogue that the Orthodox Church is able and willing to encounter our neighbor in peace and with love, regardless of the circumstance or environment.

The religious and cultural diversity that we encounter in our communities today in many ways mirrors that of the Old World centuries ago. Consequently, Orthodox Christians are called to bear witness to the love of Jesus Christ in every encounter with our neighbor. Conversely, when we encounter our neighbor with love, we glorify God by upholding Christ's commandment to "'love the Lord your God with all your heart and with all your soul and with all your mind [and to] love your neighbor as yourself.' On these two commandments hang all the Law and the Prophets" (Matthew 22:37-40). It is in embracing the relational imperative of love that we fulfill the sociality of faith.

Given this calling to embrace our neighbor in peace and love, the practical question arrives as to how we may fulfill it. This question is particularly significant given the degree to which our world is more connected, yet isolated and fractured than ever. First, we must remember that love does not require grand gestures or elevated emotions to be shared with another. The peace and love of God is most beautifully shared through a gentle gaze, a brief acknowledgment of another's presence, a smile that warms the soul. It is in these small, mundane acts that we are called to offer as gifts to our neighbor, invitations to build relationship, and signs of our desire for dialogue. The document published by the Ecumenical Patriarchate, titled *For the Life of the World: Towards an Orthodox Ethos of the Orthodox Church*, dives into this sacred principle: "Dialogue, in the Orthodox understanding, is essentially and primordially a reflection of the dialogue between God and humanity: it is initiated by God and conducted through the divine Logos (*dia-logos*), our Lord and Savior Jesus Christ. Pervading all human life, dialogue takes place in all our encounters, personal, social, or political, and must always be extended to those who adhere to religions different from ours" (par. 54).

We can also look to our spiritual leaders for inspiration and good counsel when we are faced with moments of doubt, fear, or estrangement. In the Orthodox Church, we are most blessed to have visionaries who have sought to share the peace found in spiritual freedom by building bridges of respect and love with our neighbor as opposed to walls of disdain and isolation. His All-Holiness Ecumenical Patriarch Bartholomew has been a pioneering witness in advancing the imperative of ecumenical and interfaith dialogue, manifested through the long-standing engagement of the Ecumenical Patriarchate in international ecumenical and interfaith bodies, namely the World Council of Churches (WCC)[2] and Religions for Peace (RFP), numerous theological dialogues with the Roman Catholic Church, the Oriental Orthodox Church, the Anglican

Communion, and the Lutheran World Federation, as well as consultations with Jewish and Muslim scholars and leaders. In a recent keynote address before the World Council of Religions for Peace in July 2025, His All-Holiness eloquently defines the proper posture of interfaith relations by the good fruits that come not from theological uniformity, but common service to our neighbor. His All-Holiness boldly states that:

> The true basis for common action is not the convergence on a theory, but the journeying-together in a deed. This truth is captured in the emphasis on the importance of the 'dialogue of life as a precondition for interreligious dialogue'. We meet in essence not when our theologies coincide, but when our communities share bread with the hungry, care for the sick, defend the wronged. Unity is forged in the common resistance to the forces that attempt to efface the human face. In this struggle, the diversity of our spiritual weapons is not a weakness, but a wealth. [. . .] Our unity is not founded on what we believe in common, but on our common love for humanity and on our common reference to the mystery of the one God. This is the only viable peace.[3]

Once one recognizes that interfaith relations does not involve or require a universal conformity of belief, but instead recognizes that humanity shares in one common life, in one common yearning for communion with God and neighbor, we can do nothing else but to serve our neighbor and embrace them as our friend. It is this spirit of solidarity and closeness with one's neighbor that we seek to cultivate among the faithful and in the parishes of our Archdiocese. When a fruit of inner, spiritual freedom, this spirit of solidarity and love for our neighbor can withstand and even flourish when tested by the evils and suffering of our world. This truth is most acutely evidenced in the life of our Archdiocese following the destruction of St. Nicholas Greek Orthodox Church on September 11th. As the only house of worship destroyed on that fateful day, our Archdiocese and the St. Nicholas community remained resolute in our effort to rebuild. With the consecration of the new church in 2022 and the revitalization of its community in the subsequent years, St. Nicholas Greek Orthodox Church and National Shrine stands today as a beacon of hope, a testament of the triumph of love and freedom over hatred and oppression. Functioning as an Orthodox Christian parish, a national memorial shrine, and a venue for ecumenical and interfaith prayer and dialogue, St. Nicholas National Shrine is a symbol to all that our search for freedom and love is found when we encounter the true depth of God's love for humanity and share that love with our neighbor.

While an immense challenge, this is the state that Christ calls all to: "that you love one another as I have loved you" (John 15:12). Let us then embrace this calling, being confident that God may grant us faith and discernment to be bearers of his love, spiritual sight to see him in our neighbor, and unrestrained joy in sharing our life with our fellow man.

11

An Orthodox Priest in Interreligious Dialogue

Peter Anthony Baktis

Seminary

My interfaith dialogue journey began in the early 1980s as a seminary student at St. Vladimir's Orthodox Theological Seminary. St. Vladimir's was one of five seminaries (Jewish Theological, General Theological, Union Theological, and Saint Joseph's Seminaries) that participated in an interfaith dialogue hosted at the Jewish Theological Seminary in New York City. We met once a month in the evening on an agreed common topic of scripture, tradition, or current issue central to all. Each seminary panel was to present their theological position and then a period of dialogue and inquiry ensued. This was a formative part of my theological education where I was challenged to look at my own theological tradition in the context of a wider hermeneutic while sharing not only common scriptural texts, but a new cultural worldview context that not only my Orthodox Christian tradition was living, but all of our traditions were living in the

United States of America. Interfaith dialogue was what later would be coined as "Receptive Ecumenism."[1] The members of the dialogue did not come to prove, convert or coerce. We gathered to learn from each other, share our own deep struggles in searching how to live our faith, as well as to enrich the theological traditions we represented. For me it was also a means to help me understand the transformative love of God.

Military Chaplain

Graduating from St. Vladimir's Seminary and continuing my studies at the General Theological Seminary, I continued to participate in ecumenical and interfaith dialogues. In 1985 I was ordained to the priesthood and served two parish assignments, The Cathedral of the Protection of the Holy Virgin NYC, and St. Nicholas in Jamacia Estates. In 1990, I was commissioned as a chaplain in the United States Army and began what became a twenty-five-year service. The foundation that I had from my participation in interfaith dialogue was essential in my ministry as a chaplain in the Army. I not only had to minister to soldiers of various religious traditions, but I also had to work and support my colleagues who were endorsed by various religious traditions. In addition, it was a time of great change and conflict in the world, and I found myself having to be part of teams that met and looked for solutions with religious leaders in Bosnia, Kosovo, Iraq, and various other deployments.

It was during that time that Samuel Huntington's work *The Clash of Civilizations and the Remaking of World Order* (1996) was published. Later, Secretary of State Madeleine Albright would write in her book, *The Mighty and the Almighty: Reflections on America, God, and World Affairs* (2006), how religion and religious thought was critical in world affairs and diplomacy. These two works changed the course of diplomacy for many years. As a chaplain in the Army, I was right in the middle of this new worldview that now tried to understand and include religious leaders in the sphere of influence for change and conflict resolution. My role changed, as Army chaplains were shifted to prioritize advising the Command on matters of religion. We were called to meet with religious leaders, hold briefings for our commanders and leaders on the religious backgrounds of the countries we were deploying to and to hold conferences that brought religious leaders from various traditions together to find solutions to the conflicts we were facing.

The Orthodox Church and Interfaith Dialogue

The Orthodox Church has shown not only an openness to interfaith dialogue, but its history reflects its indigenous presence for many centuries in countries and cultures that have at their core communities and citizens of other faiths (e.g., Egypt, Lebanon, Israel, Iraq, and others). It is from this rich experience that for the past twenty-five years I have represented the Orthodox Church in America at the National Council of Churches Interfaith Convening Table. My participation allowed for a non-Western Christian worldview to be represented among the many colleagues who come from several Western Christian traditions. What became apparent to all who attended and participated in the various interfaith dialogue is that, just as Christianity is not monolithic, so neither are the Islamic and Jewish traditions. At times, this diversity has made the dialogue interesting and somewhat challenging, especially for those who want to reach some agreement or consensus to draft a statement.

As an Orthodox Christian, attempting to live the orthodox Phronema,[2] consonant dissonance is a common reality.

As Orthodox Christians there is much that we can explain about the nature of God, and yet there is much unknown. The Gospels seemingly may contain differences among the four books, and on Holy and Great Friday we do not shy away from these divergences and read all four accounts of Christ's passion. In the hymnology of the Orthodox Church, we often express this consonant dissonance by asking: Why? or How? "How can a women give birth and yet remain a virgin?" "How can the uncontainable be contained in a womb?" I felt rather comfortable in the cacophony of the interreligious dialogue.

Pastoral Conclusions

Participating in interfaith dialogue has enriched my pastoral ministry. It has allowed me to be open and listen to the concerns of the members of my congregation facing difficult decisions, and the reality of living in a complex and multifaith country. I have not closed the door to participate in interfaith gatherings in our community and have joined my voice to the discourse on issues that face all our religious leaders. Interfaith dialogue allows me to listen and learn in order to strengthen not only my faith but ways in which I can also strengthen and enrich others.

Practicing Receptive Ecumenism, within the context of interfaith dialogue, builds bridges, not walls, where we can understand our differences, share respect for each other and find ways of living the words spoken to us by Christ: "'Love the Lord your God with all your heart and with all your soul and with all your mind and with all your strength.' . . . 'Love your neighbor as yourself.' There is no commandment greater than these" (Mark 12:30-31 NIV).

12

Baptists, Interfaith Relations, and "The World-Christian Turn"[1]

Raimundo C. Barreto

While the Baptist movement originated in Europe and the United States, Baptists are now present in six continents. Some of the world's largest Baptist conventions and unions are currently located in countries like Nigeria, India, and Brazil. As Baptist principles and identity are reinterpreted around the world, understanding the various ways of knowing and being that emerge from contemporary Baptist experiences across the globe is imperative. This chapter focuses on examples of Baptist experiments with interfaith relations in diverse world contexts. By situating this conversation within the burgeoning field of World Christianity, the chapter sheds light on the impact of the "World-Christian Turn," a recent historical juncture in which the demographics of Christianity are drastically changing, and Christian studies are now under the aegis of a polycentric *oikoumene,* on Baptist life and interfaith practices.[2]

Multifaith Collaboration and Interfaith Relations

Baptists are diverse people, who hold a variety of views on interfaith relations. While many Baptists continue to embrace exclusivist views on God and salvation, others seek to build bridges with other faith traditions, acknowledging the existence of common ground, thus providing a basis for dialogue. Such bridges have been built, among others, based on the fact that most faith traditions contain some version of the Golden Rule in their moral codes. As Paul Knitter highlights, people from different faith traditions often agree "on the necessity of resolving conflict nonviolently, of overcoming human suffering due to poverty, of protecting those who cannot protect themselves, of basing all socioeconomic development on an ethic of planetary or ecological responsibility."[3] One specific example of this in Baptist life can illustrate this sort of motif.

Following the killing of a Sikh-American entrepreneur, Balbir Singh Sodhi, in a suburb of Phoenix in the wake of the 9/11 attacks, American Baptist pastor Paul D. Eppinger, then the executive director of the Arizona Ecumenical Council, mobilized the council to stand in solidarity with people of other faiths. Synagogues and a Hindu temple had also been vandalized. After those tragic events, the Arizona Ecumenical Council formed an interfaith coalition. The mission statement of the new interfaith council read: "Our mission is to build bridges of understanding, respect and support among diverse people of faith, through education, dialogue, service and the implementation of the Golden Rule."[4] The Golden Rule was the organizing principle used to engage other faith groups. The twelve faith groups that formed the new interfaith council jointly declared: "We will expand our own rewarding InterFaith experience by bringing diverse people of faith together to personally discover, experience and live the richness of InterFaith dialogue, service and harmony."[5] They agreed to work together on interfaith initiatives, such as conferences and educational programming, as well as social services like housing programming and hunger alleviation. The faith groups forming this interfaith council included Bahá'ís, Buddhists, Confucianists, Hindus, Muslims (including adherents of Sufism), Jains, Jews, Scientologists, Seculars, Sikhs, Taoists, and multiple Christian denominations. All of them had a version of the Golden Rule in their traditions.[6] That common ground became the basis for their interfaith collaboration.

People from different faith traditions often come together to collaborate on issues of common interest without, necessarily, engaging each other in theological dialogue. Coalitions formed strictly to advocate for common interests are often called multifaith networks. The Washington, DC-based International Religious Freedom Roundtable, founded in 2010 and later turned into a hub for IRF roundtables around the world, exemplifies this form of multifaith coalition.[7] The IRF Roundtable describes itself as "[A] safe space where NGOs, individuals, and government officials from all faiths and none work together for freedom of religion or belief globally" (International Religious Freedom Roundtable).[8] The Baptist World Alliance (BWA), American Baptist Churches, 21Wilberforce, and the Ethics and Religious Liberty Commission of the Southern Baptist Convention (SBC) are examples of Baptist organizations that have participated in that roundtable. The IRF Roundtable responds to concerns raised by its participants by launching multifaith initiatives, publishing letters and statements, engaging in advocacy projects, and creating working groups on named issues. What unites its participants is their common interest in protecting religious freedom. They are not interested in moving toward interfaith dialogue.

By contrast, the participants of the Arizona Interfaith Movement (AIM) mentioned earlier not only shared advocacy projects but also engaged in dialogical interfaith relations. Starting locally, AIM gradually connected with other interfaith networks, including the Parliament of World's Religions.[9] At one point, Eppinger became a member of the Parliament's Board of Directors. He also participated in the Baptist-Muslim Dialogue Task Force that planned the first North American Baptist-Muslim Dialogue. Furthermore, he represented the American Baptist Churches (ABCUSA) on the National Council of Churches' Interfaith Relations Commission. Some multifaith efforts can turn into interfaith dialogue. Others will not.

The Impact of "A Common Word"

The 2009 National Baptist-Muslim Dialogue stemmed from a sense of deep solidarity that later turned into an interfaith dialogue. In its search for mutual understanding and peaceful coexistence, a "dialogue allows two parties to accept each other as they are and invites conversation aimed at understanding without the intent of changing the other."[10]

The North American Baptist-Muslim Dialogue stemmed from an ecumenical trip to Lebanon sponsored by the National Council of Churches USA in response to hostilities involving Israel and Hezbollah in southern Lebanon in 2007.[11] On October 13, 2007, the Baptist World Alliance received a letter from a group of Muslim leaders and scholars, which followed an open letter this same group had sent to Pope Benedict XVI.

The Muslims' initial open letter reacted to Benedict XVI's speech at the University of Regensburg in September 2006 on the first anniversary of the Muhammad Caricature cartoons crisis. In that speech, the Pope had portrayed Islam as "a violent religion and that the root cause of its violent nature lies in the character of the Muslim God."[12] "A Common Word" offered a reasoned response to key points of the Pope's Regensburg speech, highlighting the "prohibition of compulsion in religion," while reminding Benedict XVI that, since Vatican II, the Church had recognized that Christians and Muslims worship the same God.[13]

An expanded version of the letter, *A Common Word Between Us and You*, was sent to various Christian leaders, eliciting several Christian responses, including one from the BWA. Signed by 138 Muslim scholars, *A Common Word Between Us and You* focused on the two commandments considered equally central to Muslims and Christians: the love of God and the love of neighbor.[14] At a time when anti-Muslim discourse was increasing in the West, that document sparked an alternative narrative to *The Clash of Civilizations* by asserting that Christianity and Islam were both founded on the common principles of loving God and neighbor.[15] Accordingly, "those values provide fertile ground for creating a common life together," offering "a way forward based on interfaith engagement."[16]

The initial Baptist response was penned by David Coffey, BWA President and one of the twenty-seven world Christian leaders directly addressed in that open letter. He welcomed the Muslim letter "as a groundbreaking initiative which could make a major contribution to a better understanding in Christian-Muslim relations, the cause of religious liberty and global peace."[17] Coffey's response was followed by a formal letter from the Baptist World Alliance on December 19, 2008, addressed to Prince Ghazi Bin Muhammad Bin Talal, President of the Royal Aal al-Bayt Institute for Islamic Thought.

The BWA letter reaffirmed the "double command to love God and neighbor as being at the heart of the message of Jesus Christ as recorded in the Gospels," uttering a "yes" to the Muslim invitation to "come together" and "live in peace, respect and kindness." The letter also expressed desire for collaboration "wherever possible, in local projects for peace, justice and the giving of aid to those who are suffering and in need," concurring with "A Common Word" in that "future dialogue between us can be based on the 'common ground' of our obedience, within our own faiths, to the double love command, together with our fundamental confession of the unity of God."[18]

At the same time, the Baptist letter underscored the limits of the common ground between the two faiths, underlining that the whole range of their beliefs about God and the world could not be reduced to that double commandment. They constructed the double commandment of love of God and love of neighbor, though, as "a space or area ('ground') in which we can live together, talk with each other, share our experiences, and work together for the flourishing of human life," exploring "the eternal truths to which our respective faiths bear witness," and acknowledging that it provided "sufficient overlap between the way Christians and Muslims speak about love of God and humanity for us to understand each other and open ourselves to mutual exploration."[19]

Differences between Muslims and Christians should not be minimized. However, based on their respective sacred scriptures and their common Abrahamic roots, the Baptist World Alliance welcomed the process of exploration, recommending face-to-face conversations also on the local or regional levels. The three North American Baptist-Muslim dialogues that followed embodied the BWA recommendation for "regional unions and conventions of churches to engage in joint conversations and practical projects for aid and development with their Muslim neighbors, in ways that are appropriate for their own area."[20]

In 2009, 100 Baptist and Muslim leaders from all parts of the United States met at Andover Newton Theological School. In that meeting, they stated together, in "A Declaration of Common Will":

> Acknowledging that our respective scriptures require us to live as neighbors, we jointly pledge that we will:
> 1. Work to eradicate stereotypes and develop friendships with one another through dialogue that reflects a willingness to listen and a desire to learn;
> 2. Affirm the full integrity of one another's faith, honoring our differences and building upon our common values;
> 3. Realize that as we learn about our neighbors' faith, we enrich our own;
> 4. Cooperate together on projects that contribute to justice, peace, and the common good;
> 5. Educate our own faith communities about the importance of living together as neighbors;
> 6. Commit to pray for one another as we seek other opportunities to strengthen our friendship.[21]

This first North American Baptist-Muslim dialogue was followed by other two dialogues. The second North American Baptist-Muslim dialogue was also held at Andover Newton Theological School from November 30 to December 2, 2012, focusing on the theme "Loving God as the Pathway to Peace."

Among its speakers, Aliou Niang, a Senegalese American Baptist who practiced Islam in his early life, discussed the parallels between the Qur'an and the Bible, and how they helped him "to follow Jesus in conversation with other traditions," including African traditional religions, which also shaped his faith.[22] Citing passages from the Qur'an, rabbinic texts, and the New Testament, Niang, a Bible scholar in his own right, showed how the love of God is intrinsically connected to the love of neighbors in all these traditions. In contrast to those who use their faith to promote hatred, Niang portrayed the command to love God as an affirmation of our humanity and the basis through which one can be transformed from an enemy into a friend.

Reading the Samaritan story, which Martin Luther King, Jr., had used as the basis for his famous sermon "Loving Your Enemies" at Dexter Avenue Baptist Church in 1957, Niang dislodged Eurocentric Christianity, underscoring the wealth of non-Western Christian experiences, which are often shaped in conversation with other religious traditions.[23] His conclusion stated, "As a follower of Jesus in the Baptist faith tradition shaped by Diola Traditional Religion and Islam, I see *Loving God Whose Way Is Peace* as not a human invention but a divine vision that, when experienced, forces us to pause and expose the potential enemy within—the self."[24] In that same dialogue, Karen Thomas Smith, a Baptist chaplain at Al Akhawayn University in Ifrane, Morocco, highlighted the concept of "dialogical living," illustrating it in light of her work helping Christians to see themselves not "in opposition to Islam, but in relation to Islam and our Muslim neighbors."[25]

The Third National Baptist-Muslim Dialogue took place in Green Lake, Wisconsin, in April of 2018. Focusing on younger leaders from both faiths, this dialogue urged Christians and Muslims living in the same cities to join their counterparts in building "long-term relationships and foster mutual understanding, and, participate in a joint project to enhance the welfare of their community."[26] The idea was to strengthen relationships on the local level, examining best practices in the twinning of congregations and mosques, exploring the underpinnings of religious freedom in each tradition, and creating a provisional plan for collaboration among congregations and mosques.

In recent years, Baptists around the world have become increasingly aware of the importance of interfaith dialogue in religiously plural societies. In 2015, the scope of the BWA Commission on Baptist-Muslim Relations expanded, which resulted in its renaming as the BWA Commission on Interfaith Relations, acknowledging the diversity of Baptists interfaith experiences in distinct contexts around the world. While Baptist-Muslim dialogue remained central to its mandate, the commission at that juncture welcomed conversations about Baptist understanding of and interaction with other religious traditions. Its membership included people from Africa, Asia, and Latin America, in places where most Christians' neighbors belonged to religious traditions as diverse as Hinduism, Buddhism, African-derived religions, and other Indigenous traditional religions.

Meeting the Religious Other in *lo Cotidiano*

Ada María Isasi-Díaz promoted the concept of *lo cotidiano*, the everyday life, as the place where one can best understand God's action in the world.[27] As religion is ultimately experienced as lived faith, a focus on how religion is experienced in *lo cotidiano* can be an effective way to engage other faith traditions. Most local interfaith encounters take place in the day-to-day life of religiously plural societies. These encounters tend to start with an understanding of the participants' common humanity and happen around situations that affect community life more broadly.

In connection with understanding interfaith engagement through the lens of lived religion, it is worth noting that a number of past and present Baptists around the world live as religious minorities in their contexts. As such, those experiences have shaped the way they relate to neighbors from different faith traditions. Similar marginal social loci have, more broadly, shaped much of the Baptist ethos, principles, and theology for more than four centuries, helping them see the world from a "down-under" perspective, and stand in solidarity with other minoritized communities.[28] In tandem with that, Puerto Rican Baptist historian Luis Rivera-Pagán refers to the Bible as a literature of political dissent produced by minoritized people. Therefore, any "theology with emancipatory horizons" must truly care "about the sufferings and aspirations of subjugated peoples and victimized communities."[29] According to him, this liberationist hermeneutic helps us to see the world "from the perspective of those who suffer," promoting a sense of deep solidarity with them.[30]

Informed by such an ethos, various Baptist communities and individuals around the world continue engaging with human rights advocacy and peacemaking efforts both ecumenically and interreligiously. Daniel Buttry highlights, for instance, the work of Baptist leaders in Myanmar who have historically mediated efforts between the civil society organizations and the Burmese military government. Some of them formed groups of Christian and Buddhist leaders to mediate the demands of ethnic insurgencies in critical moments in the history of this country.[31]

The Caribbean offers another context where interfaith *convivencia* has shaped up in countries like Guyana, Trinidad, and Suriname, as Christians, practitioners of traditional religions, Jews, and Muslims have found ways to coexist in relative peace for centuries. Around 10 percent of the enslaved Africans taken to the Caribbean were Muslims.[32] Likewise, Javanese Muslims and Sanatani Hindus migrated to Suriname as indentured laborers before the turn of the twentieth century.[33] Despite the impact of religious assimilation policies, many Muslims and Hindus never converted to Christianity. While these countries are not free from tensions and conflicts that impact religious minorities, their religious communities have developed concerted efforts to promote religious diversity and a culture of religious toleration.

On the global level, the relationship between Christianity and other religions has been critical to the ecumenical agenda. At the inception of the ecumenical movement in the first decades of the twentieth century, the ecumenical ideal of Christianization of the non-Western world was problematized and nuanced in non-Western contexts. The meeting of the International Mission Council (IMC) in Tambaram, India, in 1938, provides one example of that. The significant representation of non-Western churches in Tambaram was unprecedented. The largest delegations were from India and China. As Christianity was in fact becoming a world religion, there was an increasing concern with the role of the growing churches in non-Western countries in the ecumenical movement.

In preparation for the meeting in Tambaram, Dutch historian Hendrik Kraemer wrote a book to further understanding of the Christian message for the non-Christian world.[34] Kraemer understood that evangelism and witness should be the focus of Christian relations with other faith traditions. Some Indian theologians at the meeting, though, challenged that position, arguing, first, that "Indian philosophy, culture, and tradition could not be ignored by those engaged in Christian mission on Indian soil, and secondly, that the 'Kingdom of God' rather than 'church' would provide a better platform for defining and doing mission in the pluralist context of India."[35] At Tambaram, a still incipient ecumenical movement began to realize that the increasing engagement of non-Western delegates was forcing the reimagination of the Christian relationship with the non-Christian world. The Asian churches represented in Tambaram were undergoing a process of formation in their Christian identity amidst nation-building processes that demanded their engagement in an ongoing "dialogue with religions and secular faiths within that context."[36]

Latin American Contributions to Interfaith Relations

Latin American Christians are often overlooked in conversations on interfaith relations, usually due to the misrepresentation of Latin America as a Christianized continent—the reason for its exclusion from the Edinburgh World Missionary Conference in 1910. The major missionary goal for the Indigenous population was their conversion to Christianity. Despite the evangelistic efforts that followed, Indigenous peoples and other groups targeted by colonial policies of assimilation—Jews, Muslims, and practitioners of African-derived religions—continue to be part of the Latin American religious landscape.

As Carlos Cardoza-Orlandi underscores, the Latin American Christian experience has taken place "in contexts with multiple religious alternatives—Islam, Buddhism, Hinduism, Indigenous religions, Afro Latina/o religions, *espiritismo* (Spiritism), and traditional religions."[37] One of the consequences of the interfaith interactions in such a context is the growth of fluid religious identities that combine ruptures and continuities with other religious beliefs. As Cardoza-Orlandi highlights, the "encounters, interactions, and dialogue with people, symbols, and rituals of different religions produce a new perspective, a new Christian imaginary—at times vague and at times very clear—but with a certain continuity with that which is familiar."[38]

In recent decades, Latin Americans have rediscovered Abya Yala (the Kuna name for the region) as a multireligious land. Since at least the early 1990s, Indigenous and African diasporic religions have experienced a new revitalization, sparking renewed possibilities for interreligious relations. One consequence of that new awakening to interfaith relations can be seen in the recent rise of a religiously pluralist Latin American liberation theology.[39] The justice-oriented approach it offers to interfaith relations is one of Latin America's contributions to this conversation. Theologians in other parts of the world have been inspired by it. Based on his contact with Native American and Latin American theologies, for instance, Paul Knitter came to the conclusion that "[D]ialogue must include liberation and [. . .] liberation must include the Earth, for here was a people who could not talk about the Sacred without talking about the Earth and who could not talk about the horrid sufferings they themselves have endured without talking about the sufferings of Earth and animals."[40] This paradigm for interfaith relations advances the idea of a liberating dialogue among people from different religions that focuses centrally on suffering and the need for more just relations not only among humans but also between humans and the Earth. Several Latin American Baptists, including the author of this chapter, have been closely following these recent developments in the region and actively engaging with them. A number of them, including Luis Rivera-Pagán, have played a leading role in the formation of an interfaith peace network called RECONPAZ at a gathering in Chiapas, Mexico, in 2014. While RECONPAZ is formally titled the Christian Continental Peace Network, it has intentionally engaged with other faith traditions in the Americas, particularly Indigenous and African-derived religions.

Conclusion

Although in relatively small numbers, Baptists in different parts of the world are increasingly engaging interfaith relations and making important contributions to this field. In this chapter we have briefly highlighted several interfaith initiatives Baptists have either led or been part of in different parts of the world. Though not exhaustive of Baptist views or experiences in interfaith dialogue, these contemporary examples of interfaith relations noted here coming from different parts of the world are shared in the hope that further engagement of such experiences can help us expand conceptions and approaches in Baptist life, taking into account contextual differences, including those taking place in the Global South at a time when Baptist churches are growing in the southern hemisphere. Whereas Baptist interfaith engagement takes different shapes and forms, engaging such efforts is critical to promote *buen vivir*, human dignity, and social and ecological justice, based on the integration of diverse knowledge and privileging all forms of life.[41]

13

Loving Alike: A Wesleyan Vision for Interfaith Engagement

E. Neil Gaiser

I will not soon forget the atmosphere in the room at the close of the most recent gathering of the National Sikh–Christian Dialogue in Cincinnati, Ohio. After two days of rich conversation, the gravity of our world's present moment hung heavy over us. I found myself saying what had become clear throughout our dialogue: *"What we're witnessing is the rise of a patriotism of hate—in which to love your country, you must learn to hate the other. And that is not love. That is not patriotism. It is fear, manufactured and manipulated by political powers who thrive on division."* Heads nodded around the table—Sikhs and Christians alike—because each tradition knows this reality all too well. Whether in the United States or South Asia, religious liberty is being eroded not only through law but through fear, exclusion, and the weaponization of belief. The dangers of White Christian nationalism in America mirror those of Hindu nationalism in India. The details may differ, but the pattern is painfully familiar: when religion is harnessed as a tool of political identity, neighbors become enemies, and religious minorities are often the first to pay the price.

It was not an abstract conversation for my Sikh colleagues. Their sacred history straddles borders—Guru Nanak was born in what is now Pakistan and the Golden Temple stands in India. Partition tore their spiritual homeland in two, leaving them perpetually caught between identities that politicians are all too eager to exploit. Christians in India face similar pressures, forced to prove their loyalty or be branded as outsiders. These stories struck a deep chord with me, because they reveal how easily religion can be twisted into a weapon of exclusion. Yet they also reveal why interreligious dialogue matters: it is in such spaces that we resist fear, tell different stories, and stand together in dignity.

As a United Methodist, I believe this commitment to solidarity is not only practical but profoundly theological. Nearly three centuries ago, John Wesley asked in his sermon *On Catholic Spirit, "Though we cannot think alike, may we not love alike? May we not be of one heart, though we are not of one opinion?"*[1] Wesley was speaking to fellow Christians divided by doctrine, yet his vision of a "catholic spirit" is strikingly relevant to our world of fractured faiths. In our age of suspicion and nationalism, his question becomes an urgent one: can we learn to love alike, even when we do not believe alike? For me, that is the heart of interreligious dialogue—a willingness to love the neighbor of another faith with the same seriousness as Christ commands us to love our own.

Thus, for me, Wesley's question about loving alike has become my theological grounding and starting point for interreligious engagement. In a world where religion is too often wielded as a weapon, his insistence that love outruns opinion is both countercultural and deeply Christian. The challenge, of course, is to expand his ecumenical vision beyond the walls of the church. If Wesley urged Christians to extend the hand of fellowship to one another in spite of their differences, then surely his call to a "catholic spirit" also presses us to reach toward neighbors of other faiths with the same openness. It is, after all, impossible to claim we love our neighbor as ourselves if that love stops at the edge of our own tradition.

This conviction is not mine alone. My denomination, The United Methodist Church, has long affirmed that our interreligious work is not an isolated endeavor but an ecumenical one. The National Council of the Churches of Christ in the USA, with which the UMC partners, has been building interfaith relationships for decades. In the aftermath of 9/11, the Council initiated a Muslim-Christian dialogue and expanded its work with Jewish partners into more formal conversation. In recent years, dialogues have begun with Buddhist and Hindu communities, and now, most recently, the Sikh tradition. These dialogues are unique because they are both interfaith and ecumenical. When I sit at the table, I do so alongside Christians from many denominations, learning not only from our partners of other faiths but from one another as well. This breadth of voices enriches the conversation and models the diversity we hope to see in the wider world.

Underlying these efforts is what the ecumenical world calls the Lund Principle: "churches should act together in all matters except those in which deep differences of conviction compel them to act separately." This principle challenges us to set aside unnecessary divisions and join our voices whenever possible. Applied to interreligious dialogue, it means we meet our neighbors not as scattered individuals but as a community of Christians seeking common cause. For United

Methodists, this is more than strategy—it is fidelity to our calling. We cannot credibly proclaim God's love for the world if we refuse to sit at the table with those whom God loves.

It is also important to note that this theological mandate is rooted in Scripture itself. Jesus' command to "love your neighbor as yourself" (Mark 12:31) leaves no room for loopholes, and in Matthew 25:35-40, he identifies himself with the stranger we welcome—or fail to welcome. Hospitality, then, is not an optional virtue but a core expression of discipleship. And yet, as I've preached on this Matthew passage before, such hospitality often feels uncomfortable or even threatening. It risks our security, our identity, even our certainty. That risk, however, is precisely what makes it a faithful response. The way of Jesus is never the way of fear; it is the way of open doors, shared tables, and radical welcome. When we extend that welcome across lines of faith, we do not betray the gospel—we embody it.

The scholar Paul Numrich—who was also my professor and mentor in seminary—has helpfully described three obligations that Christians have when approaching other religions. First, we must understand them as they are, not as we imagine them. Second, we must recognize the good things that are present within them. Third, we must be willing to receive critique from them.[2] I have found all three of these obligations to be transformative in my own journey.

I remember vividly a moment in class when I tried to make Buddhist teachings on karma fit into a Christian framework of heaven, hell, and purgatory. Dr. Numrich gently but firmly challenged me: Why not let Buddhism be Buddhism, and Christianity be Christianity, without forcing them into false harmony? That conversation became a turning point. It taught me that honoring another tradition means resisting the urge to bend it into my categories. To see others as they are—rather than as extensions of myself—is the beginning of genuine appreciation.

Receiving critique has been even harder, and even more necessary. I have sat across the table from Muslim presenters who could not fathom how Christians could worship a God who would "punish his own Son" or who would consign non-believers to eternal torment. I have heard Buddhists describe the Christian belief in God as a kind of delusion, a projection of the mind to avoid facing impermanence. These words are not easy to hear, but they have deepened my faith. They have forced me to re-examine what I believe and why I believe it. They have pushed me to move beyond simplistic formulations and toward a more mature, resilient discipleship.

But appreciation is not only about receiving critique—it is about recognizing goodness, beauty, and truth in unexpected places. Here the words of *Nostra Aetate* still ring in my ears: "The Catholic Church rejects nothing that is true and holy in these religions." I have seen the fruits of the Spirit—love, joy, peace, patience, kindness—blooming in communities that would never name them as such. I have seen it in the Buddhist practices that helped me care for my father during his illness, reminding me to live in the present moment and to treasure the time I had with him. I have seen it in the Sikh ethic of *seva*, or selfless service, as brothers and sisters show up to feed the hungry and care for the poor without asking who is worthy. These encounters do not make me less Christian. On the contrary, they call me deeper into the love of God, expanding my imagination of how God is at work in the world.

This, then, is what I mean by a theology of appreciation: a willingness to hold firmly to my faith in Christ while at the same time honoring the ways God's truth and love are at work in others. It is not relativism, nor is it mere politeness. It is a posture of humility and gratitude, rooted in the conviction that the Spirit of God cannot be domesticated by any single people, tradition, or doctrine. And it is this theology of appreciation that makes interreligious dialogue not only possible, but indispensable.

One Sikh brother shared a story that has stayed with me. During the anti-Sikh pogroms in India, he was attacked on a train simply for being who he was. Beaten and left for dead, he prayed not for revenge, but for his attackers, that God would forgive them. His testimony stunned me—not only because of his courage, but because it so clearly embodied the radical call of Christ himself: "Love your enemies and pray for those who persecute you" (Matthew 5:44). In that moment, I realized that interreligious dialogue is not just about what we Christians can give to others; it is also about what we can learn from them. Sometimes the gospel comes to us from unexpected lips, in unexpected lives.

This story also underscored something deeper: that Sikhs and Christians share a legacy of persecution. Both traditions know what it means to suffer for one's faith, to be treated as outsiders, to carry wounds inflicted by political and religious powers. In different times and places, our communities have been scapegoated, exiled, and even killed. And yet, both traditions have insisted that suffering can become the seedbed of compassion rather than hatred. To stand in solidarity, then, is not to erase our differences but to recognize that our pain, too, can be a meeting place. Solidarity forged in suffering has the potential to become solidarity for the flourishing of all.

The Sikh-Christian dialogue made clear that interfaith work cannot remain only at the level of words and theory.

Again and again, participants called us to move from "my freedom" to "our freedom," insisting that religious liberty is truly secured only when it is safeguarded for all. This shift requires more than goodwill—it demands advocacy. Dialogue that ends at the table risks becoming self-referential. But when it leads us into public witness, it becomes an act of faithfulness. Out of this gathering emerged commitments to deepen religious literacy, to expand future dialogues (including creating a new Sikh-Muslim dialogue), and to explore advocacy initiatives together. These steps remind us that interfaith encounter is not an end in itself, but a catalyst for collective action. In this sense, dialogue grows into practice: not just words, but a promise to act together for the good of all.

Interreligious dialogue, then, is not a peripheral activity for Christians in a pluralistic world. It is a faithful response to the God who meets us in Christ and sends us into the world to love our neighbors as ourselves. As a Wesleyan Christian, I understand this not as a dilution of the gospel but as an expression of it. John Wesley believed that God's grace is already at work in every human life, even before we recognize it. That conviction compels us to approach those of other traditions not with suspicion, but with appreciation. This "theology of appreciation" does not require us to deny the distinctiveness of our faith. Rather, it calls us to discern and celebrate the ways God's Spirit is already present and active in the lives of others, even when their confession differs from our own.

But theology that never takes flesh remains incomplete. The Sikh-Christian dialogue reminded us that the true measure of our conversations lies in the witness they bear in public life. To speak of religious freedom is to move from the safety of our own communities into advocacy for one another.

To share stories of persecution is to shoulder one another's burdens. And to break bread together is to commit ourselves to a common table in the face of forces that would divide us. In this sense, dialogue matures into praxis: not merely an exchange of words, but a covenant to act together in the pursuit of justice and peace.

At the heart of this covenant is solidarity. Christians and Sikhs alike carry legacies of persecution, whether through the martyrdom of Sikh gurus, the pogroms of 1984, or the long shadow of Christian complicity in colonialism and religious violence. These histories could drive us apart, each retreating into our woundedness. Instead, they can become the soil of mutual understanding. When one community suffers, the other is called to stand alongside them, not as outsiders offering pity, but as fellow sojourners who know something of what it means to be marginalized. As the apostle Paul wrote, "If one member suffers, all suffer together" (1 Corinthians 12:26). To walk this path together is to embody the very heart of Christ's call to love our enemies and to bear one another's burdens.

The work of interreligious dialogue will not end the divisions of our age overnight. Nor will it shield us from misunderstanding or even betrayal. But it does root us in a deeper truth: that the love of Christ is never confined to the boundaries of our own community. To love God is to love the neighbor—and in our global context, the neighbor is almost always someone of another faith. To embrace this calling is to move from appreciation to solidarity, and from solidarity to action.

This, I am convinced, is not an optional task for the Church, but a mark of its faithfulness. To engage in dialogue is to trust that the Spirit is already at work ahead of us and to join that work with humility and hope. In a time when religion is too often weaponized to divide and destroy, Christians are summoned to bear a different witness: one of appreciation, of solidarity in suffering, and of courageous action for the sake of our common humanity. Such a witness is not easy, but it is urgent. And it may be, in our fractured world, one of the clearest ways we can proclaim the gospel of Jesus Christ.

Bibliography

Numrich, Paul D. "Christian Sensitivity in Interreligious Relations." *The Asbury Journal* 67, no. 2 (2012): 53–66.

Wesley, John. "The Catholic Spirit." In *John Wesley's Sermons: An Anthology*, edited by Albert C. Outler and Richard P. Heitzenrater, 300–313. Nashville: Abingdon Press, 1991.

14

Interreligious Relations: An Evangelical Perspective

Don Thorsen

When talking about evangelical Christianity and interreligious relations, I am reminded of hackneyed jokes about the two being oxymoronic, that is, trying to hold together two things that are mutually exclusive. The two emphases have nothing in common, right?

Speaking as an evangelical Christian who has worked for more than twenty years in interreligious dialogue and collaboration, I have heard challenges from both sides of my participation. Evangelical colleagues and friends have wondered why I spend time in interreligious relations. Was I involved with evangelization? Missionary work? Apologetics?

I received similar questions from my interreligious colleagues and friends. Could I be trusted? Did I participate subversively in my involvements with interreligious dialogue and collaboration? More than once, I have had to explain my words, motives, and theology to those who did not think that I was a fit in their interreligious work.

In the late 2000s, I began serving on the National Council of Churches' Interreligious Relations Commission. I represented the Wesleyan Theological Society, which is one of numerous parachurch organizations that are welcomed by the National Council of Churches (NCC) in their commissions. In fact, the Wesleyan Theological Society has had representatives serve on NCC commissions since the 1980s. For more than half a decade before that time, I had served on the NCC's Faith and Order Commission.

I attended an ecumenical meeting in which someone said that ecumenism was inextricably bound up with interreligious relations. The more I thought about it, the more I agreed that both works were complementary. If I was concerned about ecumenism (and I am), then I needed to be concerned about interreligious relations. Thus, I participated in both of the NCC commissions and I continue to do so.

Although evangelical Christianity and interreligious relations seem incongruous with one another, both benefit through participation in dialogue and collaboration because of the knowledge they gain, wisdom they develop, and common good they accomplish. Let me begin by talking about what it means to be evangelical, especially since the moniker has become increasingly conflict-ridden. I will continue by talking about why evangelical Christians seem so averse to interreligious relations. I will give biblical reasons for why I participate in interreligious relations, giving Scripture references that are important to me as an evangelical Christian. I will conclude by talking about what I have learned and how I have matured from my interreligious relations and, perhaps, what others may learn from my experiences.

Evangelical Christianity

I grew up in a Free Methodist Church, and the denomination had been an early member of the National Association of Evangelicals. So, I had some idea about what it meant to be evangelical at an early age.

In 1976, the cover story of *Newsweek* magazine declared the "Year of the Evangelicals," highlighting the evangelical Christianity of soon to be elected President Jimmy Carter.[1] The magazine helped to popularize the term *evangelical* (or *evangelicalism*). Prior to that time, many people had talked about the fundamentalist/modernist controversy of the early part of the twentieth century as defining Christians in the United States. However, Christians affiliated with the National Association of Evangelicals, for example, Billy Graham, wanted evangelical Christianity to represent a middle way between the reactionary theology of fundamentalist Christianity and the progressive theology of modernist Christianity.

Over time, evangelically oriented Christians became increasingly conservative, religiously and politically. It became less desirable to be known as fundamentalists and more desirable to be known as evangelicals.

Recently, evangelical Christians have become emboldened in imposing their beliefs and values on American society. There has always been a kind of dominion theology at work among American Christians.[2] However, the dominionism has increased especially among evangelical Christians, and we now sometimes call it Christian nationalism. In my opinion, Christian nationalism is very dangerous, and I served on a Theology Task Force, which functioned as a subcommittee of the Interreligious Relations Convening Table. In the Task Force, we wrote a rough draft policy statement about the dangers of Christian nationalism. In 2021, the Governing Board of the NCC published the following: "The Dangers of Christian Nationalism in the United States: A Policy Statement of the National Council of Churches."[3] The statement does an excellent job of defining what Christian nationalism is, and how Christians ought to resist its exploitation of biblical and historic Christianity as well as its exploitation of people in the United States, especially those who are of a non-dominant status.

In the United States today, we find ourselves in a particularly resistant environment for loving one's neighbor as oneself (e.g., Mark 12:28-34), for doing to others as you would have them do to you (e.g., Matthew 7:12; Luke 6:31), and for generally being a friend to those not like you, including those from other religions. Why is there so much resistance?

Why Evangelicals Are Averse to Interreligious Relations

Speaking as an evangelical Christian, I am not going to cite quantitative and qualitative studies in order to talk about why my fellow evangelicals are averse to interreligious relations. As I mentioned in the introduction, evangelical Christians highly value evangelization, missionary work, and apologetics. These practices are good in my opinion. I affirm witnessing in both word and deed; otherwise, how would our children and others learn about God, Jesus Christ, and the Holy Spirit? There have been evangelists, missionaries, and apologists throughout church history, starting in the first century. Problems with these practices arose not so much because the aforementioned ministries were being done, but how they were being done. In this regard, I distinguish between evangelization and proselytism, the latter having to do with "inappropriate or unjust (and unloving) ways of doing it."[4]

Alongside the primacy of evangelization, evangelical Christians emphasize the uniqueness of Jesus Christ. In emphasizing this uniqueness, they fear betraying Jesus just by considering other religions' beliefs and values.

Evangelical Christians also fear relativism, and anything that suggests that faith is less than certain. They want to believe in the objective, absolute truth revealed in Scripture. They do not want to hear about postmodernism, nonfoundationalism, contextualization, and deconstruction, in addition to the historical and critical study of Scripture. However, they forget that they are saved by grace through faith (Ephesians 2:8-9), and that faith by definition acknowledges the presence of uncertainty.

Why I Participate in Interreligious Relations

When I first started participating in ecumenical and interreligious work, I commented on the paucity of Scripture references, at least in ecumenical documents. Ecumenical documents would start out with quotes from past converging documents, for example, or quotes from well-known ecumenists. If ecumenists wanted to attract evangelical readers, though, then I said it would help to cite early on biblical rationales for what they promoted. Too many of my ecumenical colleagues scoffed at what I said, saying that my desire for biblical references was naïve, gratuitous, narrow-minded. Did not all of their ecumenical work presume a biblical foundation? Perhaps, I said, but it would not hurt to state biblical precedents more often than not.

It is important to me to have clear biblical precedent for why I participate in interreligious dialogue and collaboration. Let me share a few biblical ideas that are important to me for my decades of work on behalf of interreligious relations. If my rationale sounds simplistic to you, then so be it. However, if you want to promote interreligious dialogue and collaboration, then you always need to be ready to give a biblical explanation (or defense) for what you promote (for example, see 1 Peter 3:15).

The most important biblical principle to me has to do with the so-called Greatest (or First) Commandment:

> One of the scribes came near and heard them disputing with one another, and seeing that he answered them well he asked him, "Which commandment is the first of all?" Jesus answered, "The first is, 'Hear, O Israel: the Lord our God, the Lord is one; you shall love the Lord your God with all your heart and with all your soul and with all your mind and with all your strength.' The second is this, 'You shall love your neighbor as yourself.' There is no other commandment greater than these." (Mark 12:28-31)

If I want to love my neighbor as myself, then I first need to dialogue with my neighbor. If I want to progress in getting to know, understand, and communicate effectively with my neighbor—even if it is with the intent of evangelizing my neighbor—then I need to be willing to collaborate with them in matters having to do with being neighborly.

Similar to the Greatest Commandment is the so-called Golden Rule. Scripture refers to it in the following way: "In everything do to others as you would have them do to you, for this is the Law and the Prophets" (Matthew 7:12; cf.

Luke 6:31). If I want people to speak with me and to collaborate with me, then I must treat them the same way. Interestingly, most religions of the world affirm a similar principle.[5]

There are other biblical rationales, of course, for encouraging interreligious relations. Since all people are created in the image of God, the *imago Dei* (Genesis 1:26-27), there exists an equality and mutuality among people. Every person, regardless of their religious affiliation, possesses a unique dignity and worth.

Many evangelicals such as myself are increasingly engaged in social justice and humanitarian work. Interreligious dialogue and collaboration are often vital to these efforts. The Hebrew Scriptures (Old Testament) are filled with injunctions to promote justice and to resist injustice (e.g., Micah 6:8; Jeremiah 29:7). In the Christian Scriptures (New Testament), Jesus notably defined his ministry by quoting Isaiah in his hometown of Nazareth:

> He [Jesus] stood up to read, and the scroll of the prophet Isaiah was given to him. He unrolled the scroll and found the place where it was written:
> "The Spirit of the Lord is upon me,
> because he has anointed me
> to bring good news to the poor.
> He has sent me to proclaim release to the captives
> and recovery of sight to the blind,
> to set free those who are oppressed,
> to proclaim the year of the Lord's favor."
>
> And he rolled up the scroll, gave it back to the attendant, and sat down. The eyes of all in the synagogue were fixed on him. Then he began to say to them, "Today this scripture has been fulfilled in your hearing." (Luke 4:16b-21)[6]

Jesus did not envision his ministry only for the sake of bringing "good news" (or evangel) to people. He emphasized the need to care for the poor, for those who are held captive, for those who are blind, sick, and injured, and for those who are oppressed. These verses inspire us to pursue peace and justice.

What I Have Learned as an Evangelical Christian

Much of what I have learned from my years of work in interreligious relations did not so much involve new learning as much as it involved substantiating what I already know. I know, for example, that all people are created in the image of God. However, in getting to know people from other religious traditions, my knowledge of them became more personal, more intimate, more instructive.

As an undergraduate student at Stanford University, I majored in Religious Studies. I did a great deal of comparative religious studies, and I knew about other religions in theory. When I intentionally sought out opportunities to engage one-on-one with people of other religions, my empathy and compassion toward them increased. I made interesting friends, had provocative conversations, and found ways to contribute to our common good.

Too often my evangelical colleagues and friends have considered the concept of a "common good" to be a temptation into thinking that people must make the world better, when only God can make it better. Although God may ultimately be the one to make the world right, so to speak, that does not exempt Christians from living Christlike lives in the present.

Realistically speaking, we as evangelical Christians do not have a choice in becoming more practiced in loving our interreligious neighbors as ourselves. We work with them. We live next door to them. We witness the marriages between people of other faiths and our own family members—an aunt or an uncle, a cousin, a daughter or a son. In an increasingly multiracial, multiethnic, and multilingual world, there are pragmatic—if not also biblical and theological—reasons for becoming more engaged with people in other religious traditions. We cannot not avoid relating with people of other religions no matter how hard some people, including evangelical Christians, try to do so. In an increasingly diverse world, we need to learn to live with one another, rather than try to segregate and in other ways discriminate against them.

I still promote witnessing to others. How can one avoid being a witness? As the saying goes, "Preach the gospel at all times, and if necessary, use words."[7] We cannot not be witnesses on behalf of Jesus Christ, if we claim to be Christian. The saying above suggests that living a life of faith and compassion, and of dialogue and collaboration, is a crucial way to share the gospel, with spoken words serving as a necessary tool when appropriate.

I have become more persuaded by ways that Christians historically have talked about inclusivism, that is, about ways by which people may be saved who have never heard of Jesus Christ or who may have never heard the gospel in understandable ways. Such people represent billions in number, which includes people who lived both before and after the time of Jesus. Many Christians believe in what is known as exclusivism, that is, that no one will be saved who does not explicitly name the name of Jesus as their Savior and Lord (e.g., John 3:36; Acts 4:12). Although many Christians have affirmed exclusivism, including Catholic and Protestant Christians, many others have believed that God provides salvation in extraordinary ways for those who are unevangelized, so to speak. Such views have been variously described as inclusivism.

For example, some Christians believe that opportunities are universally given to people to be saved during this lifetime, perhaps through dreams, visions, or angelic visitations, while other Christians believe that God will save people according to their conscience, based on what the apostle Peter said in Acts 2:12-17. Still others think that postmortem evangelism will occur, whereby people after death will have the opportunity to be saved by the atoning work of Jesus Christ.

There are pluralists, even among evangelical Christians, believing that God will ultimately save all people (e.g., 1 Timothy 4:10; 1 Corinthians 15:22). Some believe that Jesus Christ's atonement was necessary for there to be universal salvation; others do not. Realistically, few evangelical Christians believe in universal salvation, though they may find inclusivist views appealing. Still, such an appeal would not deter their emphasis on evangelization. Although one may hope for inclusivist options for the salvation of all people, the surest way of salvation occurs by responding to the gospel message of Jesus Christ.

Final Thoughts

As an evangelical Christian, I love both God and my neighbors as myself—individually and collectively, whether they are Christian or not. In particular, I pursue opportunities to dialogue and collaborate with people of other religions. In the world, we benefit from engaging in ways to dialogue, understand, empathize, and cooperate with one another. These engagements are especially important, since there seems to be a growing amount—both among Christians and non-Christians—of divisiveness, scapegoating, and discrimination against people, including the targeting of non-dominant religious people. I think that my fellow evangelical Christians have too often been at the forefront of bigoted and hateful words and of actions against people of other religions. Instead, they would benefit personally and spiritually as well as relationally and societally by becoming more involved with interreligious dialogue and collaboration. While evangelical Christianity and interreligious relations may sometimes seem at odds, engaging in dialogue and collaboration actually benefits both, as they exchange knowledge, cultivate wisdom, and jointly work toward the common good.

PART 4

Pathways for Living in an Interreligious World

15

The Witness of Interreligious Relations

Elizabeth Eaton

In 2014 I was invited to address the annual convention of the Islamic Society of North America (ISNA). This is the largest gathering of Muslims in North America, and it brings together Sunni and Shia, embodying the spirit of Ummah. Though there are aspects that are particular to Islam, the annual convention bears a remarkable resemblance to the assemblies and conventions of many Christian traditions including my own, the Evangelical Lutheran Church in America. There are featured speakers, vendors, and workshops. One in particular caught my attention—"Unmosqued to Mosqued: How to Get the Young Muslim Back to the Masjid." We've all been there.

The ISNA convention opened with a Boy Scout color guard who were given the command, "Proudly post the colors of the United States of America." They could have been a Scout troop from any community in the United States. And they were proud. We all recited the Pledge of Allegiance. This was quintessentially American.

Tifereth Israel, the only synagogue in Ashtabula, Ohio, was right next to the last parish I served. They would use our parking lot on the High Holy days, for bar and bat mitzvahs, for Channukah, and for Passover. Often the congregants would invite the community to join them for these celebrations. On the first night of Passover after the Haggadah, the traditional Seder meal, wine, singing *Dayenu*, and the declaration "Next Year in Jerusalem!" the celebration always concluded with the congregation singing "God Bless America." Also quintessentially American.

This was always the promise of the United States however imperfectly or unevenly realized. In 1790 George Washington wrote to the Touro Synagogue stating that the country gives "to bigotry no sanction, to persecution no assistance" and established that religious freedom is an inherent natural right, not an indulgence. Article VI of the Constitution makes plain that "no religious test shall ever be required as a qualification to any office or public trust under the United States." The First Amendment makes clear that "Congress shall make no law respecting an establishment of religion or prohibiting the free exercise thereof."

The United States is a multireligious, multiethnic, pluralistic experiment. There are ninety languages spoken in the homes of the school district where I live. Our grocery stores have Kosher and Halal sections. Our neighborhood is not unique. Now, more than ever, diversity is the norm across the country and monolithic communities are more rare. We live together, work together, go to school together. One would hope that such proximity would foster understanding and cooperation.

For seventy-five years the National Council of the Churches of Christ in the USA has been a vehicle to support this ecumenical understanding and cooperation. It models reconciled diversity. The vision is not to blur the distinctiveness of member churches but build on their strengths. It is unity, not uniformity. Together members engage in theological discernment, pastoral care issues, and advocacy. We do this work together, though it is not without challenge. In a society that increasingly wants to divide groups and even individuals into homogenized atomized islands, the conciliar model stands as a witness to cooperation and is stronger for it.

In the 2000s the NCC saw the need to engage others beyond the Christian traditions. The first two national dialogues—Jewish/Christian and Muslim/Christian—were established in the early 2000s. In 2018 three more national dialogues were convened—Hindu/Christian, Buddhist/Christian, and Sikh/Christian. Dialogue builds understanding and understanding builds relationships. We have found that when we engage authentically with each other as our true selves connection can be achieved. Watered-down-lowest-common-denominator dialogue is not only unhelpful, it is dishonest.

There is a debate about who is a "real" American and who is eligible to participate in social and civic life. With the rise of White Christian Nationalism, anti-Semitism and anti-Muslim violence have been legitimized. Fear and distrust are instruments of division. The point is to determine who is "in" and who is "out."

Interreligious work counters this. The Shoulder to Shoulder Campaign begun in 2010 brings together an interreligious coalition whose mission is "Standing shoulder to shoulder with American Muslims. Promoting American values." Instead of giving in to the force of division, the campaign draws on the strength of its members. In today's zeitgeist this is countercultural. It is also a reason for hope.

I began this essay with two stories of religious groups who have been othered by elements in US culture and who are experiencing hate and violence. Even though they see themselves as American, White Christian Nationalism, flagrantly promoted by members of the current US administration, would deny them any standing in civic life, disturbingly by elected and appointed officials, who took an oath to uphold and defend the Constitution. Apparently, they have neither read the First Amendment nor Article VI of the Constitution. Anti-Semitism and anti-Muslim violence gain more media attention, but other religious traditions are also discounted. And, truth be told, many Christian traditions, including member churches of the NCC, do not qualify as legitimate.

This is why interreligious engagement is not merely academic or theoretical, it is essential. If one of our voices is stilled or one of our traditions erased we are all the poorer for it and equally at risk. Interreligious relations are not only a pathway to greater understanding and therefore deeper relationships, but also to a deeper understanding of our own traditions that leads to honest authentic engagement.

16

The Middle East and Interfaith Relations: Intersections and Challenges

Peter Makari

Local and global events often have a direct impact on interfaith relations, seemingly more negatively than positively. For relations among people of the three Abrahamic faiths—Judaism, Christianity, and Islam—realities in the Middle East, especially Palestine and Israel, weigh particularly heavily, whether explicitly or not. At this writing, after almost three years of unconscionable war and destruction in Gaza and the region, the intersection of interfaith relations and world events is perhaps more palpable than ever, and the need for free and honest dialogue is necessary. My own personal and professional engagements have informed my involvement in such dialogue and have heightened my awareness of these intersections, beginning from an early age.

Growing up in a rather large Midwest capital city, I had the privilege of attending a college prep school, graduating in a class of sixty-four students. Having attended the same school since third grade, I knew most of my classmates well from interacting a lot in class, participating in extracurriculars including sports, and socially. Our school was independent, meaning it was not grounded in any particular faith tradition, and so religion was neither part of the curriculum nor explicitly part of the atmosphere or culture. Even so, it is safe to say that my class was predominantly Protestant and Catholic Christians, with about eight or nine Jews, one Hindu, and probably some of other traditions, and unaffiliated or not-practicing. But again, faith was not a prominent feature in our interactions, despite some awareness of religious diversity and observance of traditions, particularly as the school provided special lunches for Jewish students during Passover, and when we turned thirteen, I remember attending classmates' bar mitzvahs. (It was a boys' school at the time.) Our class was mostly White European, but with a few students of different southern and east Asian and other heritages. I believe I was the only one in our graduating class with Arab-Middle Eastern roots—I the son of an Egyptian father (a Presbyterian minister) and a White Euro-American mother (also Protestant and theologically educated).

In my lower and early middle school years, my closest friend was Michael. We did a lot together. I still have a picture from his bar mitzvah and remember vividly being invited to his family's home for Passover Seder. It was special for me to share with Michael's family in observing the ritual as Michael's friend and their guest. Before going, I re-read the story of Passover, which provoked me to think about its setting in Egypt, elements of my own heritage of which I was proud, and the role of the pharoah as oppressor of the Israelites.

During my fifth-grade year, the Camp David Accords were signed between Egypt and Israel. In homeroom after the Accords had been announced, I made a comment about how Egypt and Israel could now be at peace. I have never forgotten the immediate and curt response of one of the Jewish students in my class (not Michael) who said, "We will never be at peace!" At the time, I was caught off guard and taken aback. He had made the political news personal—including himself and me in his statement—associating Israel with his Jewish identity. I had not made the connection between Judaism as a faith observed by my schoolmates and the State of Israel, so the comment caused in me a new awareness of Jewish affinity with modern Israel. From my perspective until then, my Jewish classmates went to synagogue on sabbath and Hebrew School on Wednesdays like I went to church and Sunday school on Sunday. Now, a new set of questions arose in my mind.

* * *

A little over ten years later—having graduated from college—I had moved to Egypt to begin graduate school. I was in Cairo at the beginning of the US-led war to expel Iraq from Kuwait in 1991. Returning to the US a few weeks after the start of the war, I could sense acutely the attitudes in this country about the Middle East—a heightened awareness of the region now that there were US troops on the ground, but also a generalizing and caricaturizing oversimplification of the peoples, cultures, and (mis-)understanding of Islam, designed to fit into the mainstream commercial media's coverage of the war. (There were few sources of alternative media at the time, such as social media.) That coverage, of course, was more heavily focused on military strategy and progress toward tactical goals, but at the same time, it ignored or dehumanized the people, and reduced to caricature the context of Iraq and the Middle East. The war was declared over in 100 hours, but ideas of Islam replacing Soviet communism as the new enemy of the US were beginning to become more prevalent. Just a decade later, the attacks of September 11, 2001, resulted in the so-called "war on terror" whose physical theaters were Afghanistan and Iraq, but psychologically more broadly, "the Muslim world."

In 2000, I had begun as staff for the Christian Church (Disciples of Christ) and United Church of Christ, responsible for our partnerships in the Middle East and Europe. Throughout this past quarter-century, I have observed how issues of and realities in the Middle East have directly affected the practice and content of interfaith relations, especially between Christians and Jews and Christians and Muslims. In my professional role, I have had the chance to participate in efforts to address how this intersection has been manifested.

Following the 9/11 attacks, and throughout the lead-up and execution of the US-led invasions of Afghanistan and Iraq, I received numerous and regular invitations to speak in different settings of the church about the Middle East and Islam. It was a "teachable moment" in the US, to speak about Islam and Muslims in the world—their faith and their diverse practices, and on the history of the modern Middle East, including the impact of US policies since American global ascendance following World Word II. Even though most of the world's Muslims are not Middle Eastern, and not all Middle Easterners are Muslim, there has always been an automatic (and negative) association of the two categories, which was especially pronounced after 9/11. I learned that patience and nuance are important and that people of faith in our church communities were eager to learn and go beyond stereotypes, to offer solidarity, and to advocate.

In the broader US culture, "Islamophobia" was building and there was a clear desire among our churches to deepen understanding and reject a posture of animosity. A year after Pope Benedict XIV spoke at the University of Regensburg in Germany in a speech that offended Muslims around the world, "A Common Word Between Us and You" was published by prominent global Muslims as an invitation to the world's Christian leaders to join in dialogue and action. "A Common Word" highlighted the shared principles of both faiths: love of God and love of neighbor. Efforts in the US to re-invigorate dialogue between Christians and Muslims were exemplified by a 2007 initiative, of which I was privileged to be a part, to re-constitute national Muslim-Christian Dialogue through the National Council of Churches and American Muslims. That initial meeting in Dearborn, Michigan, led to the establishment of the Muslim-Christian Dialogue table that continues to meet today. The issue of Islamophobia (incorrectly named, in my opinion) and the impact of American foreign policy, especially in the Middle East, on American Muslim communities have been topics on the agenda.

At the same time, discussions about the possibility of an American interfaith coalition to counter anti-Islam bias and anti-Muslim attitudes and actions led to the creation in 2010 of the Shoulder to Shoulder Campaign. Shoulder to Shoulder is "committed to ending anti-Muslim hatred, discrimination, and violence" in the US and has been active over this decade and a half to "connect, equip, and mobilize" concerned people of faith to counter anti-Muslim sentiment.[1] Through providing opportunities for personal interaction and solidarity, attitudes have changed, even though the work remains as critical as ever fifteen years after its launch.

The conflation of interfaith relations and international relations from the highest levels of US government, including the White House, has persisted throughout the first quarter of the twenty-first century. Days after 9/11, George W. Bush visited the Islamic Center of Washington, delivering remarks in which he affirmed Islam as a religion of peace and spoke of Muslims' positive contributions to American life. In the same week, however, he had spoken of the US's war on terrorism as a "crusade." That war has been geographically located, initially in Afghanistan and Iraq but later in other parts of the Middle East like Sudan and Yemen, and as a result, connected the people of those countries with "terrorism." Domestically, also in 2001, Congress passed the USA PATRIOT Act which has been instrumentalized to implement measures of surveillance, control, and detention in the domestic "war on terror," primarily against US Muslims and people of Middle Eastern and South Asian heritage, advancing a dangerous dichotomy of animosity between the US and Islam.

This dichotomy was furthered as Barack Obama contended with assertions that he is Muslim, due to his father's Kenyan nationality and his own middle name, Hussein. In a debate during the 2008 presidential campaign, candidate and then Senator John McCain responded to an audience assertion that Sen. Obama is "Arab" and "I can't trust him," by saying, "No ma'am. He's a decent family man, a citizen that I just happen to have disagreements with on fundamental issues, and that's what this campaign is all about."[2] The late Senator McCain notably had not dismissed the questioner's slur against Arabs, and by extension, Muslims.

During his first inaugural address, President Obama promised a "new way forward, based on mutual interest and mutual respect"[3] with the so-called Muslim world. He sought to fulfill that promise with his speech titled "A New Beginning" at Cairo University on June 4, 2009, following outreach to Muslim and Arab leaders. Framed as a speech to the "Muslim world" and on "US-Muslim relations," Obama spoke extensively on US policy in the Middle East, especially on Israel-Palestine, perpetuating the conflation of the Midde East and Islam, even though most of the world's Muslims do not, in fact, live there, and not recognizing that US policy in the region affects Middle Eastern Christians and others in significant ways as well. By focusing so extensively on the realities of the Middle East, Obama disregarded the realities of Muslims in other parts of the world, including the US, setting them apart from the societies and nations in which they live. Despite these flaws, the speech was seen as a positive overture to Muslims and to the Middle East, articulating ideas that had not been stated so clearly by a US president on US policy and realities in the Middle East, especially in the post-9/11 era.

Donald J. Trump, in the first few weeks of his first term, signed Executive Order 13769, "Protecting the Nation from Foreign Terrorist Entry into the United States," which is more commonly known as the "Muslim ban." Extended a year later by a second such order (EO 13780), the policy implication was restriction of travel to the US by foreign nationals from mostly majority-Muslim countries, mostly in the Middle East. This action signaled an especially restrictive Trump policy on immigration, consistent with a White Christian nationalist ideology that has marked Trump's two terms in office. Many Americans, including Christians, have worked tirelessly against the ban and the ideas behind it, but the policy and ideology have pervaded both of Trump's terms so far.

* * *

It is not a stretch to assert that the defining issue in the Middle East for over a century has been Palestine and Israel, a crisis that has borne directly on interfaith relations in the US for some time. Since October 2023, special attention has been afforded it, including Palestinian Lutheran theologian and pastor, Rev. Dr. Munther Isaac's suggestion that Gaza is the "moral compass" of the world. However, the impact—and the history—spans the last century. US policy in support of Israel for much of that period has been consistent, virtually unconditional, and uncritical.

From a US policy point of view, in between Trump's first term as president and his current term, Joe Biden's interaction with the Middle East was marked by his (and Congress's) unwavering support for Israel in its assault on the Palestinian people in Gaza and belligerence in the wider region. Throughout his career, Biden has always been open about his affinity and solidarity with Israel, and since October 2023, that translated into tens of billions of dollars in arms sales and military assistance to the country, diplomatic support at the UN, and the contradictory articulation and conduct of US foreign policy in the concurrent wars in Russia-Ukraine and Israel-Palestine.

Predating 2023, though, issues of Israel and Palestine have been divisive in an otherwise productive and positive atmosphere in Jewish-Christian dialogue. Topics such as occupation, the use of economic measures (including boycotts, divestment, and sanctions, including restricting US military aid to Israel—a position now supported by many Democrats in the Senate), Israeli apartheid, settler colonialism, and now genocide have proven difficult when addressed, at least, and have caused ruptures in these relationships. Some rich discussions about Christian Zionism, Palestinian liberation theology, and religious nationalism have taken place over the years, including the time since October 2023. However, limiting the focus to shared condemnation of the Hamas attacks of October 7 and the necessity of the release of Israeli hostages sets aside Israel's killing of tens of thousands of Palestinians, massive displacement, and near-total destruction of Gaza since October 2023 on the one hand, and the longer history and context of oppression that Palestinians have endured on the other. Meaningful dialogue about these topics and others like the right of Palestinian self-determination, state and structural violence, and Jewish attitudes toward Israel (including Zionism) must be afforded adequate space, as dialogue at its best is about going beyond points of intersecting views to engage matters of potential and real disagreement, in which differing perspectives and points of reference can be brought authentically and openly to the table. Too often, discussion of the Middle East in interfaith dialogues has meant a choice between engaging the difficult realities and preserving a relationship by avoiding them, but the two should not be mutually exclusive.

Such critical positions have caused tension in spaces of interreligious dialogue, but honest and authentic presence is what is expected and necessary for true engagement. Our churches have attempted to remain committed to interfaith dialogue by standing with American Muslims and Jews when incidents of anti-Muslim bigotry and antisemitism occur, and at the same time remaining faithful and clear in our critique of US policies in the region, such as militarization. A poignant example of such accompaniment was a meeting of the national Jewish-Christian Dialogue in 2018 in Pittsburgh, Pennsylvania, just a year after the Tree of Life Synagogue shooting, which included a visit to the synagogue and sessions on antisemitism. Even so, superimposing notions of antisemitism and Islamophobia on Middle East politics only exacerbates an oversimplified narrative, and for Christian churches, ignores and negates Middle Eastern Christian voices and the deep and long-standing relationships North American churches have with Middle Eastern Christians.

* * *

In reflecting on years of engagement on Middle East issues, personally, academically, and professionally, it is easy to identify times when matters of political policy and global and local events have impacted—often negatively—interfaith relations. The effects have been especially noticeable in relations among the three Abrahamic faiths—Judaism, Christianity, and Islam—which are predominant and are rooted in the Middle East. Volumes have been written on specific cases and political, economic, and social, history; I could not begin to cover the full scope of those in this chapter and have only just named a few. Yet the commitment to engage has often (but not always) prevailed, even when uncomfortable.

When I lived in the Middle East, I was immersed in the realities of interfaith relations there firsthand. There, such interfaith encounters are a natural element of life that people experience at a conscious or subconscious level. It is manifest in the use of language, in styles of dress, in practices of ritual prayer and worship, celebrations of holidays, and in deliberate dialogical engagement, and cannot be separated from daily life. Common life is not always easy, but is necessary and real, and a fact. Formal dialogue between leaders of different religious sects often weaves worldly topics with theological explication and vice versa. Ideas of governance, citizenship, human and legal rights, conviviality, and social cohesion are often grounded in scriptural and theological ideas to find common ground.

Such deliberate efforts to address social issues and promote better relations are necessary in the US today as well. When US society is as politically polarized as it is, and when religious identity can be a source of exclusionary discourse and hatred, we must persist in honest and open dialogue, coming to the table with conviction and authenticity, but also with an openness to hearing the others who are there. We can draw on the lessons of those in other parts of the world, including the Middle East, who have deep and long experience in interreligious engagement, to seek a more just world, and not resign ourselves to suggestions of perpetual and unresolvable conflict. Speaking in the Israeli-Palestinian context, to paraphrase the Rev. Dr. Mitri Raheb, eminent Palestinian Christian theologian and Lutheran pastor, religion has too often been part of the problem; but it can also be part of the solution. Open and honest interfaith engagement has, can, and should continue to draw on our religious traditions and principles to seek justice and resist the systems of oppression in a fragmented and polarized world, perhaps most especially in the Middle East.

17

Faith Beyond Boundaries: Reclaiming Pluralism in an Age of Christian Nationalism

Paul S. Tché

Introduction: The Changing Religious Landscape of North America

The United States and Canada are among the most religiously diverse societies in the world. Over the past half century, the assumption of a "Christian nation" has steadily eroded as people of many faiths—and those of none—have shaped public life. This shift challenges long-standing institutions but also offers rich opportunities for cooperation and shared purpose across traditions.

At the same time, a powerful counter-movement has emerged in the form of Christian nationalism, which fuses religious identity with national identity. It claims that the United States is, or should be, a Christian nation and that Christianity deserves cultural and political dominance. In practice, this ideology privileges one narrow version of Christianity—often aligned with whiteness, patriarchy, and political power—while excluding others.[1]

Christian nationalism undermines the democratic promise of equality, justice, and religious freedom. The Constitution's guarantee that no single religion should rule public life stands directly opposed to this movement's aims. Christian nationalism seeks to reshape civic life around sectarian authority, threatening both faith and democracy.

By contrast, religious pluralism offers a hopeful and constructive alternative. Pluralism is more than tolerance; it is the *active* effort to understand, respect, and collaborate with people of different beliefs. It calls for humility, fairness, and shared commitment to the common good. In a pluralistic society, faith deepens through encounter, and community flourishes through diversity.[2] The religious pluralism provides the necessary theological and ethical framework to effectively confront and dismantle the exclusive, divisive claims of Christian nationalism in North America.

I. The Roots and Dangers of Christian Nationalism

To see why pluralism is essential and is the appropriate response, we must first acknowledge how deeply Christian nationalism is woven into the American narratives. From the earliest colonial encounters, religion was used to justify domination and even the power of empire—erasing Indigenous traditions and blessing systems of enslavement and segregation. Though the Constitution enshrined freedom of religion, that promise was not equally extended to all.

Christian nationalism draws from this legacy. It presents Christianity as the only true faith and the nation as divinely chosen, treating other religions—and even other Christian expressions—as threats to be overcome.[3] This mindset divides communities and fuels fear and resentment.

Periods of social change often intensify such exclusionary impulses. When people feel anxious about shifting identities or power structures, rigid forms of religion can offer a false sense of certainty. Across traditions, this pattern is familiar—but when linked with nationalism, it becomes especially volatile. Christian nationalism is not merely a theological claim; it is a political project that uses faith language to sanctify hierarchy and control. It transforms religion from a source of compassion into a weapon of division. The core danger is that political interests hijack religious beliefs, exploiting religious sentiments for ethnic or political ends, leading to explosive, polarizing situations. Christian nationalism is the political manifestation of this religiously sanctioned tribalism.[4]

II. Religious Pluralism: Toward a Community of Mutual Belonging

The pluralist ideology offers a complete philosophical and practical pivot away from the exclusivist mindset. Religious pluralism moves beyond mere tolerance—defined as simple acceptance or "not minding" that others exist. Instead, pluralism demands mutual respect and understanding, solidarity, and creative cooperation in common pursuits, driven by a consistent pursuit of social harmony and authentic love in practice.

The pluralist vision is grounded in several crucial concepts:

A. Humility Before the Mystery of God

Theological pluralism is a philosophical and historical conviction that acknowledges the multiplicity of the world's religious life. This perspective stems from the belief in a sovereign Ultimate Reality (God) who cannot be contained within one culture or tradition, revealing itself through many culturally and historically differentiated ways. Pluralists recognize that there are many revelations and paths to salvation, forcing the abandonment of the assumption of Christian superiority and absoluteness in salvation claims. The necessary disposition for all participants is humility, seen as the essential attribute for genuine dialogue.[5]

B. Embracing Religious Hybridity

North America's diversity has also produced new forms of multiple religious belonging, where people draw meaning from more than one tradition. While not universally accepted, this phenomenon reminds faith communities that spiritual identity can be fluid and creative.[6]

Such hybridity carries insight and power:

- It challenges rigid boundaries and unsettles the notion of a rigid Christian identity, showing that faith can be lived in many ways.
- It empowers the marginalized, who can reclaim agency and resilience through multiple sources of wisdom.[7] It can function as a strategy of resilience and resistance against dominating systems. It will allow for the creative appropriation of various religious and cultural sources. This is particularly relevant given the history of racism and structural oppression woven into the US landscape.
- It points toward an open vision of church and society, one that values cooperation over conformity.

Pluralism, then, is not about dilution but about deepening—discovering a wider, more compassionate imagination of faith and community.

III. Justice as the Moral Center and the Unifying Core

For pluralism to counter Christian nationalism effectively, it must be rooted in ethics and action. Its credibility depends on the pursuit of justice.

A. Shared Humanity and Common Values

Nearly all faiths affirm that every person possesses inherent dignity. In both Christian and Islamic thought, this belief—sometimes called theological anthropology—sees humanity as sacred, created with purpose and worth. Love for one's neighbor, extended without condition, forms the moral foundation of coexistence. Pluralism is thus not an abstract idea but a way of life grounded in compassion, fairness, and solidarity.

B. The Work of Repentance and Renewal

Authentic pluralism begins with honest self-reflection. Every religious community must confront its own failures—moments when it has caused harm or remained silent in the face of injustice. For Christians, this includes confessing participation in slavery, colonialism, and the suppression of other faiths.

Repentance here means more than remorse; it is a transformation of heart that leads to new behavior. This process of repentance (a change of heart) and critical self-reflection is essential to overcome the inherent fears and self-sufficiency that preclude sincere dialogue. It requires leaders to boldly articulate a prophetic and critical word within their own communities concerning inconsistencies and omissions. Therefore, it also requires rejecting proselytism (coercive conversion) as a violation of human freedom. True dialogue honors conscience and allows each person to follow their own spiritual path without coercion.

C. The Prophetic Role of Justice and Dia-praxis

The credibility of religion, and thus the strength of the pluralist counter-ideology, is determined by a firm commitment to peace and non-violence.[8] Religious traditions are called to be the voice of the voiceless and the power of the powerless. To achieve real and lasting impact, the pluralist effort must embody dia-praxis—moving beyond abstract theological encounters (dialogue of words) to practical engagement (dialogue of deeds or life) for the promotion of social justice and human dignity.[9]

The critical agenda items where this shared action must occur in North America include addressing systemic issues like racism, social injustice, economic development, international justice, poverty, human rights, and the environment (ecology). Dialogue is vital when its participants actively share their lives together, seeking a just community for humankind.

IV. Building a Culture of Pluralism for Implementation and Sustained Resistance in North America

The effective confrontation of Christian nationalism requires sustained, localized efforts based on pluralist principles, transforming American civic life from the grassroots up.

A. Cultivating Authentic Interfaith Dialogue

Dialogue must be understood as an essential requisite for the honorable and conscientious citizenship of the human family. It is a truth-seeking and community-building conversation that requires participants to define themselves freely.

1. Building Trust and Mutual Appreciation: Dialogue must be conducted in an atmosphere of mutual trust and acceptance. It facilitates a better appreciation of the fundamental aspects of the religious experience of others. Instead of suppressing differences, dialogue requires listening and honestly recounting and interrogating disagreements.[10]
2. Hospitality as a Political Act: The practice of hospitality involves inviting the stranger into one's private space, converting hostility into acceptance, and recognizing mutual gifts.[11] Christians are called to radical hospitality—a welcoming engagement with the other—as part of their vocation. This move is crucial in the North American context, where interfaith organizations can mobilize people to bring about change, greatly enhancing the "power of faith for good."[12]
3. Challenging Fundamentalism: Moderate religious leaders, particularly Christian leaders, must engage in interreligious dialogue to address and counter the rise of aggressive fundamentalist forces within their own traditions.[13] This internal critique is a precondition for credible interreligious engagement.

B. Education and Institutional Transformation

To solidify pluralism as the dominant ideology, intentional pedagogical strategies are required across all levels of society.

1. Teaching for Pluralism: Educational initiatives must equip students and citizens with skills for pluralism—including active listening, empathy, perspective-taking, and

curiosity-building—to enable constructive engagement across deep differences. This approach applies pluralistic frameworks to real-world issues through case studies and bridge-building practices.[14]

2. Reforming Religious Education: Theological training and religious education in churches and seminaries must be revised to eliminate materials that encourage fanaticism (excessive, single-minded, religious zeal), and insensitivity.[15] Leaders must be prepared to live in a permanently interfaith and religiously pluralistic world.[16] The goal is to cultivate an appreciation of other religious traditions, not merely to promote shared values. Religious leaders should see diversity as an expression of unity of humanity.
3. Community Building: Dialogue must be localized into the "dialogue of neighbors," moving from intellectual pursuit to a shared culture of action in everyday life.[17] Local initiatives, such as interreligious councils and shared efforts on community problems, demonstrate that interreligious and intercultural relations are an integral part of community and family life in the USA. This community building requires acknowledging diversity and genuinely respecting the freedom of each person's conscience and human rights.

When lived out daily, pluralism becomes more than theory; it becomes a culture of relationship and respect.

Conclusion: The Vision of a Just and Hybrid Future

The exclusive claims and divisive tactics of Christian nationalism threaten the moral and civic fabric of North America. Religious pluralism confronts this danger not by minimizing faith but by widening its reach—rooting belief in love, humility, and justice.

This vision calls Christians and others to move beyond their own boundaries and to work alongside people of different traditions, trusting that God—or the sacred mystery—may also be at work in them. Dialogue, understood as both a spiritual journey and a public commitment, becomes the means of transforming this vision into reality.

By embracing complexity, pursuing justice as the shared calling, and recognizing multiple religious belonging as a sign of resilience and creativity, religious pluralism offers a path toward a more humane civilization—one grounded in dignity, solidarity, and peace. It invites North Americans to transform hostility into hospitality and to build, together, a commonwealth of compassion that extends beyond borders, beliefs, and fears.

18

How to Stay Human: Cruelty, Beauty, and Moral Leadership Today

Michael Reid Trice

Introduction

As leaders across plural, religious, civic, and private sectors, we aim to see the world truly. Today we are presented with patterns of cruelty now become ordinary in daily life. Cruelty is often evident in the *systems* and their suppositions that govern society, in the *institutional* production of diminishment: patterns of speech, policy, and power that withdraw recognition from the vulnerable and train a society to treat that withdrawal as normal.[1]

This essay treats cruelty as a systemic danger baked into the structures that govern daily life, about which religious and wisdom traditions have long warned. And yet these traditions also tell a story of humanity's capacity to resist and even to flourish amid cruelty.[2] The formative power of beauty—which I clarify below—can likewise shape us and influence our inner dispositions, our habits and behaviors, our way of leading in the world each day.

This essay also extends an earlier line of inquiry beginning in 2006, in which I described cruelty as a fracture running through intrapersonal, interpersonal, and institutional life.[3]

Five Features of Cruelty

To see cruelty clearly, I name five features of cruelty that help us see its formation at work.

First, cruelty is most visible at its extremes—war crimes, overt hatred, public humiliation—but it rarely begins there. It starts with small diminutions of recognition: the cutting side comment about a person or group, the "harmless" stereotype, the slow erasure of voice in institutional contexts where systems govern our lives. These moments often appear ambiguous enough to be minimized or dismissed. They feel like a vibration in the bones more than a blow to the face. Václav Havel describes how people "live within the lie" by learning to accommodate early distortions of truth.[4] Cruelty in systems is quiet at first; tyrants cultivate self-doubt across institutions as part of the machinery of aspirational dominance.

Second, cruelty rarely knocks on our front doors seeking admittance. It enters laterally, clothed in the language of ethics, moral conviction, law, and public policy. Friedrich Nietzsche helps name this moral "bait-and-switch" through what he called transvaluation.[5]

Transvaluation unfolds in two movements. First, inherited values—and the policies that embodied them—are dismissed as harmful and then stripped of moral authority. Next, new values and policies are enacted, often using the same language, but reinfused with contrary moral aims. Recent political efforts to redirect the US Department of Justice Civil Rights Division's enforcement priorities toward alleged fraud—without evidence—risk erasing decades of commitment to combating discrimination in voting, housing, employment, and disability access. Transvaluation is not merely the replacement of one value with its opposite; it is more destabilizing than that. It skews the moral field like a fun house mirror, confusing the public conscience, disrupting the moral barometer of individuals, and wreaking havoc within society.[6]

Cruelty's disguises do more than justify harm; they also aim to disorient the public's capacity to reason and to judge. Part of cruelty's interior deceit is that it foils rationality itself. Yet this bewilderment is not accidental. Cruelty frequently operates by manufacturing implausibility—by pushing actions beyond the horizon of what reasonable people expect—so that moral attention is exhausted in confusion. In such conditions, the question is no longer simply, *Is this right?* It becomes, *Is this even real?* The ruse succeeds when it fractures both moral clarity and rational coherence, leaving the public suspended between disbelief and resignation, and ultimately trained to accept the unacceptable.[7] Cruelty, in these ways and more, becomes not only an outward harm but also an inward discipline: a formation of the self in the image of domination.

Third, the topic of internalized cruelty opens a way of observing it across three atmospheric rivers that converge in daily life.

1. The *intrapersonal river* involves the turning of hostility inward. Here the human being becomes accuser, judge, and

punished subject simultaneously. Self-contempt, internalized racism or misogyny, and shame constitute powerful forms of intrapersonal cruelty. They deform our moral aperture and distort self-perception.

2. The *interpersonal river* describes cruelty between persons. This river includes bullying, humiliation, gaslighting, and the weaponization of difference in everyday life. It is the domain most commonly acknowledged, although it remains inseparable from the other two.
3. The *organizational or institutional river* is the most consequential. Here cruelty is embedded in bureaucratic procedure, economic systems, algorithms, law, and habituated social exclusions enacted through policy. It is impersonal, routinized, and therefore scalable.

Cruelty fourthly invites mimicry. It is inherently contagious across the three rivers identified above. In any of these cases, often the most natural response to violation is retaliation, which may promise short-term satisfaction yet reproduces the very logic it claims to resist. In this way, those in power will use cruel ends to clinch the system around individuals and communities, for instance by claiming and quelling insurrection through escalations of cruelty that were fabricated by those controlling the system in the first place.[8]

James Baldwin's observation that "the fire begins in the heart" is apt.[9] Retaliation stokes the same inner flames cruelty relies upon to justify itself. Refusal of cruelty's grammar is an act of disciplined moral freedom; refusal opens alternative moral possibilities that cruelty is incapable of fathoming for the individual or for the world.

Renée Nicole Macklin Good's death in Minneapolis in January 2026 names the point with painful clarity: cruelty does not merely act; it interprets. It seeks to monopolize meaning by making violence appear necessary, and by converting the victim into the author of her own harm. In the days that followed, Good was spoken of in the abstract grammar institutions reach for in moments of public scrutiny—threat, compliance, justification, procedure—as though a human being could be reduced to the categories required to excuse what happened. This is one of cruelty's most reliable strategies: after the wound, the narrative; after the force, the rationale.

Finally, cruelty's aim is relational rupture. It seeks to isolate persons from one another and from themselves. In institutional life, this may take the form of choosing the new veneer of national "rightness" over community relationship. As noted above, exclusion is frequently justified precisely in the name of moral or doctrinal purity.[10] The antidote to cruelty is not merely better argumentation. It is the restoration of trust, belonging, and mutual recognition.[11] It is the slow reweaving of what Wendell Berry calls "the neighborly covenant."[12] This does not mean ignoring injustice; rather, it means insisting that the pursuit of justice itself remain humanizing. Where relationship is renewed, cruelty loses one of its primary aims: the fragmentation of the human world. And where recognition is restored, cruelty loses one of its primary instruments: isolation.

Beauty Binds

If cruelty fractures, beauty binds. Beauty is a way of perceiving, inhabiting, and shaping the world such that life becomes more intelligible—and more bearable. Across religious and philosophical traditions, beauty has been associated with order, radiance, balance, and depth of meaning. In the register of this essay, beauty is closer to O'Donohue's claim than to mere aesthetic taste: it is that in whose presence we feel more alive. And if, as Arendt warns, evil's danger is its rootlessness—its limitless drift—beauty is one of the ways human beings re-root one another in the world, restoring limit, texture, and moral intelligibility where cruelty has tried to dissolve them.

First, beauty arises from recognition. Recognition is the opposite of the bureaucratic gaze: it refuses to treat a person as a case, a risk, a problem to be managed.[13] In the long migratory record, *connection* was the condition of endurance. Fire circles functioned as a social technology: the site where a "we" was repeatedly remade through story, shared food, and attention to the vulnerable. This is why connection is our prevailing thesis.[14]

Second, *meaning* is the architecture of beauty. Beauty is experienced when values, narratives, and practices cohere in a way that renders existence intelligible and worthwhile. Individuals feel beauty when their lives rhyme with their deepest convictions; communities experience beauty when their structures, practices, and purposes align.

This suggests that human beings can endure extraordinary hardship when they perceive that their suffering participates in a story larger than private distress. Meaning transforms endurance into vocation.

Early human pathways forged through ancient migrations required more than logistics; they required a cosmology sturdy enough to interpret drought, death, birth, fear, and awe—and a telos resilient enough to keep the group from dissolving into mere self-preservation.[15]

Third, *coherence* is not perfection. It is integrity across the parts of a life. Where institutions preach one thing and practice another, dissonance erodes credibility and morale. Where communities embody their professed commitments, coherence is experienced as a form of aesthetic rightness—things "fit."

Martin Buber described this movement from "I–It" to "I–Thou," where the other is encountered not as object but as person. Beauty and coherence are generated whenever human beings relate to one another in genuinely dialogical ways.[16] The migratory analog is concrete: a people survives long routes through patterned coordination—roles held in trust, discernment repeated day after day, small adjustments made without abandoning the shared aim. Coherence is what keeps plurality from becoming chaos. Felt beauty is between the inner conviction and outer action, between speech and practice, between the human claim "you are a thou" and the institutional habit of treating people as an it.

Fourth, *limit* is frequently misunderstood as the opposite of beauty, yet it is its precondition. A rose is beautiful not despite its brevity but because of it. The knowledge that a moment will not return intensifies attention to it.[17] Historically, migrating peoples, refugees, and communities under duress often create astonishing beauty. Their limit conditions sharpen perception. Songs, prayers, and artistic forms arise not to deny suffering but to interpret it.

Some of the most beautiful moments occur at the edge of loss: sitting with a dying friend, acknowledging the end of a vocation, or sensing one's own diminishing strength. Limit invites gratitude rather than possession; it teaches reverence. Beauty in the presence of limit becomes a disciplined attentiveness to the preciousness of the finite—and, in a time when cruelty so often tries to make the world feel disposable, that discipline becomes one of beauty's most quietly resistant forms.

In such conditions, leadership becomes a moral vocation steeped in both discernment and associated action: the work of safeguarding the human world—its dignity, its shared reality, and its relational integrity—against the slow corrosion of transvalued virtues and routinized harm. This practice of discernment and action belongs not only to religious leaders. It belongs to leaders across plural, public, and private sectors wherever decisions are made that shape the lives of others.[18]

The response required is not a call for leaders to "be nice." It is the disciplined practice of beauty as moral resistance: the cultivation of the conditions in which human beings can remain human together. In an age when cruelty presents itself as virtue and confusion becomes a strategy of control, leadership must reestablish the moral and relational conditions that cruelty seeks to dissolve.

Four Practices

Four practices are therefore urgent.

Connection - The first moral task of leadership is to restore visibility: to insist, publicly and institutionally, that no human being is exhaustively describable by the role a system assigns them. This is not simply interpersonal warmth. It is institutional design. It is whether policies presume dignity or presume suspicion; whether workplaces reward truth-telling or reward silence; whether communities are structured to protect the vulnerable or to manage them as risk. Connection is the moral practice of recognition. Leaders who practice connection create conditions where people can appear as persons rather than as instruments, abstractions, or liabilities.

Meaning - Second, cruelty does not merely act; it interprets events and often judges the powerless. It seeks to monopolize meaning by making violence appear necessary and by converting the victim into the author of their own harm. In this way, cruelty does some of its most durable work after the wound: it produces the rationale, the procedural language, the "justification" that allows institutions to preserve their innocence. Cruelty continues as a self-reinforcing cycle of harm.

Leaders today must therefore become stewards of moral narration.[19] They name what is happening in language that refuses to disguise harm as virtue. Meaning is revived when leaders keep human lives attached to stories larger than bureaucratic categories—stories of dignity, obligation, mutuality, and shared fate.

Coherence - Third, coherence is not perfection. It is integrity across the parts of a life and across the moving parts of an institution.[20] Cruelty thrives where dissonance is normalized—where organizations claim justice while practicing exclusion, claim care while routinizing harm and toxicity, claim truth while rewarding distortion.[21]

Coherence is therefore one of leadership's most powerful moral disciplines. It requires leaders to resist the temptation to outsource responsibility to systems. It requires refusing the excuse that "the institution did it," when institutions are always carried forward through human decisions.[22] Coherence demands that values not merely be announced, but embodied—especially when doing so carries cost.

Limit - And fourth, cruelty expands when it is unbounded—when nothing interrupts it, when no reverence restrains it, when no neighborly claim is permitted to matter. Limit is therefore not the enemy of leadership; it is one of its central moral teachers.[23] Honoring limit means leaders must know where power stops. It means establishing boundaries around what cannot be done to human beings, even when the institution is anxious, even when the public demands spectacle, even when retaliation feels justified.[24]

Conclusion

Cruelty and beauty are formative teachers. Cruelty habituates people to the unacceptable until resignation begins to feel like realism. Beauty, by contrast, forms persons and communities toward life. Beauty restores the conditions of a shared world; it is the disciplined refusal to let cruelty define what is real. Connection makes persons visible again; meaning that refuses cruelty's monopoly on interpretation; coherence that aligns speech and practice; and limit that interrupts the appetite for the limitless.

The work of interreligious dialogue belongs directly within this moral vocation. At its best, interreligious engagement is not merely an exchange of ideas between traditions; it is a disciplined practice of recognizing the humanity of those whom history, politics, or theology have often rendered distant or suspect. In a world where cruelty thrives on isolation, caricature, and the withdrawal of acknowledgment and recognition, interreligious encounter restores visibility across differences. Religious and wisdom traditions have an existential obligation to contain deep reservoirs of moral language capable of resisting cruelty's transvaluation of virtue, reminding all religious communities that dignity, care, and restraint are not the property of any single tradition but are sinewed in the shared obligations of our human family. When leaders from unique religious traditions learn to collaborate for the common good, they model a form of coherence that cruelty cannot easily fracture. In this sense, interreligious engagement is itself a spiritual practice of beauty. How so? Interreligious engagement cultivates connection where suspicion and reservations might otherwise grow; it also sustains meaning across cultural boundaries, curates relational integrity among communities, and reminds us all that daily life requires limits to domination. In an age in which the machinations of cruelty are utilized to divide communities along religious and cultural lines, the work of interreligious dialogue is an essential task within our daily lives.

Finally, leadership is about formation: the shaping of attention, habits, and institutional norms that teach people what to expect from power and what to believe about one another. The question before us is not only what we will do in the face of cruelty, but what we will become—and what our religious organizations will train others to become. To practice beauty as a spiritual discipline is to refuse the world that cruelty is trying to make, and to insist—through policy, speech, relationship, and restraint—that human dignity remains real for all as the great democratizer in a world yearning for equilibrium.

Contributors

Editor
Edward E. Thompson

Associate Editors
Barbara G. Hager
Kah-Jin Jeffrey Kuan
Peter E. Makari
Don Thorsen

The Very Reverend Peter Anthony Baktis is an Orthodox priest with over forty years of experience, including twenty-five years as a US Army Chaplain (1990–2015). He has published theological articles in various journals and Army publications. Fr. Peter serves on several boards, including International Orthodox Christian Charities, the Dialogue Institute, Military Officers Association, and the New Jersey Coalition of Religious Leaders. He is CEO of Saints Cosmas and Damian Human Services. He has represented the Orthodox Church in ecumenical and interreligious forums such as the National Council of Churches and Christian Churches Together. Fr. Peter is currently Rector of Mother of God Joy of All Who Sorrow Orthodox Church in Princeton, New Jersey.

Raimundo C. Barreto holds a PhD in Religion and Society from Princeton Theological Seminary, where he serves as an associate professor of World Christianity. His publications include *Protesting Poverty: Protestants, Social Ethics, and the Poor in Brazil* (Baylor University Press, 2023) and *Base Ecumenism: A Latin American Contribution to Ecumenical Praxis and Theology* (Fortress Press, 2025). He has co-edited several volumes, such as *Theologies and Ethics of Oppressed and Marginalized People* (Wipf and Stock, 2025) and *World Christianity and Ecological Theologies* (Fortress, 2024). Additionally, he is the general editor of the Fortress Press series World Christianity and Public Religion and a co-editor for the World Christianity book series published by Pennsylvania State University Press.

The Revd Dr Clinton Bennett, OSFC, FRAI, FRAS, has worked as a Baptist missionary in Bangladesh (1979-1982), as a university chaplain and professor, and has pastored and co-pastored local congregations. He was responsible for interfaith relations at the British Council of Churches (1987-1992) and, since 2014, has represented the Alliance of Baptists on the NCCC-USA's Interreligious Relations and Collaboration Convening Table. A graduate of Manchester, Birmingham, and Oxford Universities, his publications include *Understanding Christian-Muslim Relations* (2008), *Interpreting the Qur'an* (2009), *In Search of Understanding: Reflections on Christian Engagement with Muslims* (2019), and, most recently, *Baptist Engagement with Islam* (2025).

Rev. Dr. Whitney Bodman is a United Church of Christ pastor who served churches in Massachusetts. He then returned to Harvard Divinity School for a Doctorate in Islamic Studies and Comparative Religion. He taught Comparative religion for twenty years at Austin Presbyterian Theological Seminary. He has participated in interfaith dialogue at local, regional, and national levels throughout his career. His research has focused primarily on the Qur'ān and the nature of scripture.

He currently works with the National Council of Churches and Churches for Middle East Peace.

Elizabeth Eaton was born and raised in Cleveland, Ohio. She received a Bachelor of Music Education from the College of Wooster, Wooster, Ohio, and Master of Divinity from Harvard Divinity School, Cambridge, Massachusetts. Eaton was ordained in 1981 by the Lutheran Church in America, a predecessor body of the Evangelical Lutheran Church in America. She served as a parish pastor for twenty-five years in three congregations in Ohio. In 2006 Eaton was elected bishop of the Northeastern Ohio Synod, ELCA and in 2013 was elected presiding bishop of the Evangelical Lutheran Church in America. Eaton served as chair of the governing board of the National Council of Churches 2023-2024. She is married to the Rev. T. Conrad Selnick, an Episcopal priest. She and her husband have two grown daughters and three grandchildren.

His Eminence Archbishop Elpidophoros (Lambriniadis) of America, Most Honorable Exarch of the Atlantic and Pacific Oceans, is the eighth Archbishop of America elected since the establishment of the Greek Orthodox Archdiocese in 1922. He has served as the Orthodox Secretary of the Joint International Commission for the Theological Dialogue between the Orthodox Church and the Lutheran World Federation and as a member of the Patriarchal delegations to the General Assemblies of the Conference of European Churches and the World Council of Churches. He was the Secretary of the Pan-Orthodox Synods in Sofia (1998), Istanbul (2005), Geneva (2006), and Istanbul (2008). He has been an active member of the World Council of Churches serving on its Central Committee. He also has served on its Faith and Order Commission since 1996 and currently serves as chair of the governing board of the National Council of the Churches of Christ in the United States.

Rev. E. Neil Gaiser is an ordained Elder in the West Ohio Conference of The United Methodist Church and holds a Master of Divinity with a specialization in Interreligious Contexts from the Methodist Theological School in Ohio. He serves as an Ecumenical and Interreligious Representative of the Council of Bishops and represents The UMC on the Interreligious Relations Convening Table of the National Council of Churches. He is Co-Convener of the National Sikh-Christian Dialogue and has participated in the National Hindu-Christian and Buddhist-Christian Dialogues. Neil has also served with several local interfaith organizations throughout the state of Ohio. He and his wife, Alvie, have two daughters, Amelia and Rochelle.

Rev. Barbara G. Hager was ordained to pastoral ministry in the Presbyterian Church (USA) in 1982 after graduating from Princeton Theological Seminary (MDiv) and Allegheny College (BA). She has served as pastor and head of staff in churches in Minnesota, Pennsylvania, Connecticut, and North Carolina. A practicing attorney for many years and having served on her denomination's judicial panels, Rev. Hager currently serves as Chair of the Bills and Overtures Committee of the Coastal Carolina Presbytery. She is a member of the Jewish-Christian dialogue group of the National Council of Churches. She resides in Wilmington, North Carolina, and enjoys reading, art galleries, and travel.

Darrell Jodock has a BA Summa Cum Laude from St. Olaf College, an MDiv from Luther Seminary, and a PhD from Yale University. In addition to serving a parish in Washington,

DC, he has taught at Luther Seminary, Muhlenberg College, Gustavus Adolphus College, and St. Olaf College. He is active in adult education and the author or co-author of several books. A member of the dialogue co-sponsored by the National Council of Churches and the National Council of Synagogues, he also serves on the NCC Interreligious Convening Table. He co-authored the 2019 ELCA policy statement, "A Declaration of Inter-religious Commitment."

Kah-Jin Jeffrey Kuan is Co-President and Professor of Hebrew Bible at Claremont School of Theology, where he served as President from 2013 to 2023. He previously held academic and leadership roles at Drew University, Pacific School of Religion, and the Graduate Theological Union. He holds degrees from Emory University, Perkins School of Theology, and Trinity Theological College. His scholarship centers on ancient Israel, the Book of Job, Asian hermeneutics, and biblical education. An ordained United Methodist clergy, he co-convenes the National Buddhist-Christian Dialogue and has served on several theological boards and accrediting bodies.

Rev. Dr. William L. Johnson, III, is a senior pastor at the Washington Metropolitan African Methodist Episcopal Zion Church-Saint Louis, Missouri. Dr. Johnson also serves as a board-certified hospital chaplain (APC) and manager of spiritual care services at Christian Hospital NE (BJC Healthcare) in St. Louis, Missouri. His ministry and scholarship focus on prophetic leadership, authentic voice, and faith at the intersection of personal narrative, community transformation, and public life. He has participated in national ecumenical and interreligious initiatives through the National Council of Churches and is committed to cultivating dialogue that leads to faithful witness and shared action for the common good.

Kathryn Mary Lohre serves as Chief of Staff at St. Olaf College in Northfield, Minnesota. Prior she served as the Executive for Ecumenical and Inter-Religious Relations in the Office of the Presiding Bishop of the Evangelical Lutheran Church in America, and as assistant director of the Pluralism Project at Harvard University, Dr. Diana Eck's research project on religious diversity in the United States. From 2012-2013 she served as president of the National Council of Churches USA, the first Lutheran and youngest woman. She was a consulting editor for *Engaging Others, Knowing Ourselves: A Lutheran Calling in a Multi-Religious World* (2016).

Dr. Peter E. Makari serves as Global Relations Minister for the Middle East and Europe with the Common Global Ministries Board of the United Church of Christ and the Christian Church (Disciples of Christ). He is a member of the National Council of Churches' Interreligious Convening Table, participates in national interfaith dialogue initiatives, and represents the Christian Church (Disciples of Christ) as co-chair on the Steering and Executive Committees of the Shoulder to Shoulder Campaign. An Egyptian-American, Makari has lived in Cairo, Egypt (1991-1994), and Limassol, Cyprus (1997-2000). Makari has earned an MA in Middle East Studies from the American University in Cairo (1993) and a PhD in Politics and Middle East Studies from New York University (2003).

Bishop Vashti Murphy McKenzie is a trailblazing retired bishop of the African Methodist Episcopal (AME) Church. In 2000, she made history as the first woman to be elected to the episcopacy in the denomination's over 200-year history. Bishop McKenzie further broke barriers by serving as the first woman President of the Council of Bishops and Chair of the General Conference Commission. She has presided over districts in Africa, Tennessee, Kentucky, and Texas, and is the author of six books, including *Not Without a Struggle: Leadership for African American Women in Ministry*. Bishop McKenzie is currently the President and General Secretary of the National Council of the Churches of Christ in the USA (NCC).

Rev. Dr. Laura Osborne is a minister in the Reformed Church in America. She serves in the role of Coordinator for Ecumenical Relations and Disability Concerns as a member of the denominational staff for the RCA. She is also a campus pastor with International Campus Ministry at Western Michigan University. She lives in Michigan with her husband and three daughters.

The Reverend Margaret R. Rose recently completed service as Interim Rector of St. Michael's Episcopal Church, NYC. Previously, as Deputy for Ecumenical and Interreligious Relations for The Episcopal Church, she held leadership positions in the National Council of Churches, World Council of Churches, Religions for Peace, and Shoulder to Shoulder, among others. Her work as parish priest has focused on interreligious engagement, anti-racism, peace building, and reconciliation. She studied at Wellesley College and Harvard Divinity School, with continuing studies at the Institute of Politics and Protestant Institute of Theology in Paris, University of Geneva and the World Council of Church's Ecumenical Institute. She has held positions in community organizing, feminist theology, and urban mission in Massachusetts, Georgia, and New York.

Rev. Paul S. Tché is an ordained minister in the Christian Church (Disciples of Christ) and serves as President of the Christian Unity and Interfaith Ministry (CUIM), where he leads the church's ecumenical and interreligious engagement in the United States and Canada. He also serves as General Secretary of the Disciples Ecumenical Consultative Council, the global communion of Disciples churches. A Korean-American committed to peace and reconciliation, he has been involved in efforts for just peace on the Korean Peninsula for more than a decade.

The Very Rev. Dr. Edward E. Thompson, Rector of Trinity Church, Swarthmore, and a regional dean in the Episcopal Diocese of Pennsylvania, has served churches on the east and west coasts as senior pastor and as an outside facilitator of challenging conversations. He has had a lifelong interest in multicultural settings and interreligious discourse. He holds degrees from Williams College (BA), The Church Divinity School of the Pacific (MDiv), and George Mason University's School for Peace and Conflict Resolution (PhD), where he focused on peacemaking through religions. He has participated in three of the NCC's interreligious dialogues and, as a member of the Theology Task Force of the Interreligious Convening Table, co-authored the NCC's policy statement on religious nationalism (2024).

Don Thorsen, PhD, is Professor of Theology at Azusa Pacific University. He has served on behalf of the Wesleyan Theological Society with the National Council of Churches, both in the Convening Table on Theological Dialogue and Matters of Faith and Order and in the Convening Table on Interreligious Relations and Collaboration. He co-chairs the Hindu-Christian Dialogue. Thorsen has published more than twenty books, some of which have been translated into six different languages. He writes about topics having to do with

Christian theology, spirituality, ecumenism, and interreligious relations.

Dr. Michael Reid Trice, PhD, EMBA, is the Spehar-Halligan Endowed Professor and Executive Director of the Center for Ecumenical and Interreligious Engagement at Seattle University (CEIE-SU). He is the founder of *Religica* and editor-in-chief of the online journal, *The Interfaith Observer*, both virtual and multimedia platforms that advance religious pluralism and healthy democracy in the world. The author of *Encountering Cruelty*, Trice recently co-edited two multi-author volumes with Georgetown University Press: *Gratitude, Injury, and Repair in a Pandemic Age* (2025) and *Discerning Leadership: Responsibility and Transformation* (2027). He teaches at both CEIE-SU and in the Center for Leadership Formation in Executive Leadership at Seattle University.

Notes

1. Walking Humbly: My Journey of Interreligious Engagement

1. According to Naomi Schaefer Riley, the author of *'Til Faith Do Us Part: How Interfaith Marriage is Transforming America* (New York: Oxford University Press, 2013), 6, "the rate of interfaith marriage in the United States has more than doubled. About 20 percent of couples married before the 1960s were interfaith matches. Of couples married in the past decade, 45 percent were. The 2001 American Religious Identification Survey reported that 27 percent of Jews, 23 percent of Catholics, 39 percent of Buddhists, 18 percent of Baptists, 21 percent of Muslims, and 12 percent of Mormons were married to a spouse with a different religious identification."

2. "What Is Pluralism?" The Pluralism Project, Harvard University, website, accessed November 2, 2025, https://pluralism.org/about.

3. S. Wesley Ariarajah, *Your God, My God, Our God: Rethinking Christian Theology for Religious Plurality* (Geneva: World Council of Churches, 2012), 30-31.

4. C. S. Song, "From Israel to Asia: A Theological Leap," *Theology* 79 (1976): 90-96.

5. Archie C. C. Lee, "The Creation Myth of Nu Kua and the Biblical Narrative in Genesis 1–11," *Biblical Interpretation* 2 (1994): 312-324.

2. Friendship at the Heart of Interfaith Relations

1. "America's Interfaith Infrastructure: A Summary Report (2012)," The Pluralism Project at Harvard University, October 27, 2025, https://pluralism.org/america%27s-interfaith-infrastructure.

2. The Pluralism Project at Harvard University, October 27, 2025, https://pluralism.org/about.

3. The Pluralism Project at Harvard University, October 27, 2025, https://pluralism.org/women-transcending-boundaries.

4. "Women's Interfaith Initiatives After 9/11," The Pluralism Project at Harvard University, October 27, 2025, https://pluralismarchive.hsites.harvard.edu/womens-interfaith-initiatives-united-states-post-911-2006.

5. "America's Interfaith Infrastructure: A Summary Report (2012)," The Pluralism Project at Harvard University, October 27, 2025, https://pluralism.org/america%27s-interfaith-infrastructure.

3. The Gifts of Difference: Learning to Pray

1. *Interreligious Relations with a Focus on Peace: A Policy Statement Supporting the NCC's Interreligious Priority and Reaffirming the 1999 Policy Statement 'Interfaith Relations and the Churches,"* par. 2 (October 2019, National Council of Churches). Accessed at https://nationalcouncilofchurches.us/common-witness/interreligious-relations-with-a-focus-on-peace/.

2. *Holding Difference Together: Episcopal Theological and Practical Guidelines for Interreligious Relations* (The Episcopal Church, November 10, 2023). Accessed at https://www.episcopalchurch.org/wp-content/uploads/2024/08/EIR-Holding-Difference-Together.pdf.

3. *Toward Our Mutual Flourishing: The Theological Statement* on *Interreligious Relations,* Text and Study Guide (The Episcopal Church, 2009). Accessed at https://www.episcopalchurch.org/wp-content/uploads/2021/06/eir-toward-our-mutual-flourishing.pdf.

4. See Carol Schersten Lahurd, Darrell Jodock, and Kathryn Lohre, eds., *Engaging Others Knowing Ourselves: A Lutheran Calling in an Inter-Religious World* (Minneapolis, MN: Lutheran University Press, 2016).

5. Lynette Wilson, "Boston cathedral's call to be 'a house of prayer' extends to Muslims' Friday prayers," posted October 25, 2019, ENS: Episcopal News Service, accessed at https://episcopalnewsservice.org/2019/10/25/boston-cathedrals-call-to-be-a-house-of-prayer-extends-to-muslims-friday-prayers/.

6. Margaret Rose, *"Ecclesiology and Conflict,"* ed. Robert Heany, Christopher Wells and Pierre Whalon, *When Churches in Communion Disagree* (Dallas: Living Church Books, 2022), 101-118.

4. Interreligious Work Can Heal

1. "Rwanda: The Protestant Churches and the Genocide: press release," African Rights, written and published December 2, 1998, https://reliefweb.int/report/rwanda/rwanda-protestant-churches-and-genocide-press-release.

2. See Marc Gopin, *To Make the Earth Whole: The Art of Citizen Diplomacy in an Age of Religious Militancy* (Emmaus, PA: Rodale Press, 2004).

3. For further introduction to Scriptural Reasoning and for practical resources, see the Scriptural Reasoning: Rose Castle Foundation website, http://www.scripturalreasoning.org. For those who wish to dive into the philosophical grounding and documented experience of the method in various contexts, this site also lists academic resources.

4. See https://pluralism.org, supported by Harvard University. This is an excellent website for an introduction to what the website calls "promising practices" in interreligious engagement.

5. For the Case Initiative, see https://pluralism.org/case-initiative. For specific cases, see Elinor J. Pierce, *Pluralism in Practice: Case Studies of Leadership in a Religiously Diverse America* (Maryknoll, NY: Orbis Books, 2023).

6. See Sarah Cobb, *Speaking of Violence: The Politics and Poetics of Narrative in Conflict Resolution* (New York, NY: Oxford University Press, 2013).

7. Aziz Abu Sarah continues the work of dual-narrative tours through Mejdi Tours. See Mejdi Tours, https://mejditours.com/home-mejdi/.

8. Kenneth R. Melchin and Cheryl A. Picard, *Transforming Conflict through Insight* (Toronto, Ontario: University of Toronto Press, 2009).

9. See "Insight Policing: Conflict Resolution for Law Enforcement," https://www.insightpolicing.com. For further, see Megan Clare Price, "The Process and Partnerships behind Insight Policing," *Criminal Justice Policy Review*, 27:5 (July 2016), 553-567.

10. For the seminal work grounding Insight in theology in relation to the human desire to know, see Bernard J. F. Lonergan, *Method in Theology: Volume 14* (Toronto, Ontario: University of Toronto Press, 1972).

5. "There's a Wideness in God's Mercy": My Engagement with Islam

1. Anselm of Canterbury, *Proslogion*, trans. M. J. Charlesworth (Notre Dame, IN: University of Notre Dame Press, 1979), 1.

2. Frederick William Faber wrote a hymn entitled "There's a Wideness in God's Mercy"; see Hymnary.org, website, accessed December 17, 2025, https://hymnary.org/text/theres_a_wideness_in_gods_mercy.

3. Lesslie Newbigin, *The Gospel in a Pluralist Society* (Grand Rapids: William B. Eerdmans, 1989), 119.

4. Hasan Askari, *Spiritual Quest: An Inter-religious Dimension* (Pudsey, West Yorkshire: Seven Mirrors, 1991), 90.

5. Askari, *Spiritual Quest*, 90.

6. Askari, *Spiritual Quest*, 80.

7. L. Bevan Jones, *Christianity Explained to Muslims* (Kolkata, India: YMCA, 1938), 75-6.

8. Kenneth Cragg, *The Pen and the Faith: Eight Modern Muslim Writers and the Qur'an* (London: Allen and Unwin, 1985), 109.

9. See Alliance of Baptists, website, accessed December 17, 2025, https://allianceofbaptists.org/.

7. Some Benefits of Interreligious Dialogue

1. Kathleen A. Cahalan and Douglas J. Schuurman, editors, *Calling in Today's World: Voices from Eight Faith Perspectives* (Grand Rapids: William B. Eerdmans Publishing Company, 2016).

2. See the National Council of Churches statement on "The Dangers of Christian Nationalism in the United States."

8. Life at the Intersection: Interreligious Dialogue, the Convening Table, and the Practice of Faithful Listening

1. "Interreligious Relations and Collaboration," National Council of Churches, accessed June 22, 2026, https://nationalcouncilofchurches.us/interreligious-relations-and-collaboration/.

2. "Interreligious Relations with a Focus on Peace: A Policy Statement Supporting the NCC's Interreligious Priority and Reaffirming the 1999 Policy Statement, 'Interfaith Relations and the Churches,'" National Council of Churches, adopted October 2019, https://nationalcouncilofchurches.us/common-witness/interreligious-relations-with-a-focus-on-peace/.

3. "Interfaith Relations and the Churches: A Policy Statement of the National Council of Churches of Christ in the U.S.A.," National Council of Churches, adopted November 10, 1999, https://nationalcouncilofchurches.us/common-witness/interfaith-relations-and-the-churches/.

4. Susan Neiman, *Learning from the Germans: Race and the Memory of Evil* (New York, NY: Picador Paper/MacMillan Publishers, 2020).

5. Martin Luther King, Jr., "Letter from Birmingham Jail," in *Why We Can't Wait* (New York: Signet Classics, 2000), 77-100. Dietrich Bonhoeffer, *Ethics*, ed. Eberhard Bethge (New York: Touchstone, 1995).

9. Making Safe Spaces at University for Interreligious Dialogue

1. Sallie B. King, "Chapter 8: Interreligious Dialogue," ed. Chad V. Meister, *The Oxford Handbook of Religious Diversity* (Oxford: Oxford University Press, 2010), 104.

2. Sallie B. King, "Interreligious Dialogue," 103.

3. Sallie B. King, "Interreligious Dialogue," 103.

4. Austin Flannery (ed.), *Vatican Council II: Nostra Aetate (Declaration on the Relation of the Church to Non-Christian Religions)*, (Collegeville, MN: Liturgical Press, 2014).

5. John Hubers, "Arabian Mission–1889," ed. Charles Van Engen, Jean Van Engen, and Sally Tapley, *Called to Serve: Essays on RCA Global Mission*, The Historical Series of the Reformed Church in America, No. 102 (Grand Rapids, MI: Reformed Church Press, 2020), 59.

6. John Hubers, "Arabian Mission–1889," 59.

7. Hilary Hull, "Al Amana Centre—Building Trust and Peace in Oman and Beyond" (n.d.), Al Amana Centre: Building Trust and Peace. Accessed November 19, 2021. http://www.alamanacentre.org.

8. Hilary Hull, "Al Amana Centre—Building Trust and Peace in Oman and Beyond."

9. Huston Smith, *The World's Religions* (New York: HarperOne, 1991), 236.

10. James Jinhong Kim, lecture notes, 2. [Editor's note : Prof. James Jinhong Kim currently teaches in Global Christianity and Missiology at New Brunswick Theology Seminary, in New Brunswick, NJ. See https://nbts.edu/faculty-directory/james-jinhong-kim/.]

11. James Jinhong Kim, 3.

10. Building Bridges of Hope

1. Maria Skobtsova, *Essential Writings*, ed. Jim Forest (Maryknoll, NY: Orbis Books, 2003), 19.

2. Cf. There is a trove of documents and occasions that His All Holiness was outspoken on regarding a number of critical matters, the following are merely a few more recent articles: "Message Of Ecumenical Patriarch Bartholomew for the Interfaith Dialogue 'Advancing The Responsibility To Protect The Rights And Dignity Of The Child,'" World Council of Churches, November 26, 2025, https://www.oikoumene.org/resources/documents/message-of-ecumenical-patriarch-bartholomew-for-the-interfaith-dialogue-advancing-the-responsibility-to-protect-the-rights-and-dignity-of-the-child; "Ecumenical Patriarch Bartholomew and Interfaith Harmony," Archons of the Ecumenical Patriarchate, April 1, 2025, https://archons.org/persecution/hah-interfaith-harmony/; Chris Durante, "Ecumenical Orthodox Theology and Interfaith Dialogue: Reflections on Patriarch Bartholomew's call for a 'Common Sacred Worldview,'" Public Orthodoxy, September 19, 2025, https://publicorthodoxy.org/good-reads/ecumenical-orthodox-theology-and-interfaith-dialogue/.

3. "Keynote Address by His All-Holiness Ecumenical Patriarch Bartholomew at the Meeting of the World Council of Religions for Peace (Istanbul, July 29, 2025)" Οικουμενικό Πατριαρχείο, July 29, 2025, https://ec-patr.org/29/07/11/39/keynote-address-by-his-all-holiness-ecumenical-patriarch-bartholomew-at-the-meeting-of-the-world-council-of-religions-for-peace-istanbul-july-29-2025/.

11. An Orthodox Priest in Interreligious Dialogue

1. Receptive Ecumenism is attributed to Paul Murray and his book: *Receptive Ecumenism and the Call to Catholic Learning*. Receptive Ecumenism is characterized by its commitment to critical but constructively oriented discernment in one's own community or tradition, combined with constructive yet appropriately critical

reception of other churches and traditions for fruitful growth, reparative healing, and greater Christian and human flourishing. Although the emphasis is Christian Dialogue, I find it helpful as a model for interfaith and other dialogic encounters.

2. *Phronema*, a Greek term meaning "mind," "spirit," "thought," "purpose," "will." It is used in Eastern Orthodox Theology to convey a particular mindset, outlook, or worldview. It is how one practices the faith (*orthodoxia*) in a correct manner (*orthopraxis*). See: Eugenia Scarvelis Constantinou, *Thinking Orthodox: Understanding and Acquiring the Orthodox Christian Mind*, Ancient Faith Publishing, Chesterton, Indiana, 2020. "The Orthodox phronema ("mentality," "Stance," or "approach") is the foundation of Orthodox Christianity. It is usually unexpressed and unexamined, and rarely discussed, but it affects not simply what we believe and why but—above all else—how we think," p. 15.

12. Baptists, Interfaith Relations, and "The World-Christian Turn"

1. This chapter is a shorter version of a longer essay to be published in *The Oxford Handbook of Baptist Studies*, edited by Paul F. Fiddes, David Bebbington, Elizabeth H. Flowers, and Steven R. Harmon (Oxford: Oxford University Press, forthcoming in 2026).

2. Paul Kollman, "Understanding the World-Christian Turn in the History of Christianity and Theology," *Theology Today*, 71/2 (2014) 164-177 (166).

3. Paul F. Knitter, *One Earth, Many Religions: Multifaith Dialogue and Global Responsibility* (Maryknoll, NY: Orbis Books, 1995), 69.

4. Paul D. Eppinger, "How Different Are We Really?" *American Baptist Quarterly*, 26/3 (2007): 313-325 (318).

5. Eppinger, 318.

6. Eppinger, 318.

7. Raimundo C. Barreto, "Light from Interreligious Resources," in Amy L. Chilton and Steven R. Harmon, eds., *Sources of Light:*

Resources for Baptist Churches Practicing Theology (Macon, GA: Mercer University Press, 2020), 144-157 (150).

8. International Religious Freedom Roundtable, "Who We Are and What We Do," website, https://www.irfroundtable.org/, accessed on June 9, 2023.

9. Eppinger, 325.

10. Robert E. Johnson, "Baptist-Muslim Dialogue," *American Baptist Quarterly*, 28/1 (2009): 3-4.

11. Roy A. Medley and Sayyid M. Syeed, "Baptist-Muslim Dialogue: How This Story Began," *American Baptist Quarterly*, 28/1 (2009), 5-7 (5).

12. Miroslav Volf, *Allah: A Christian Response* (New York: HarperOne, 2011), 20.

13. Volf, 26.

14. Volf, 29.

15. See Samuel P. Huntington, *The Clash of Civilizations and the Remaking of World Order* (Norman, OK: Oklahoma University Press 1996).

16. Eboo Patel, "A Common Word vs. Clash of Civilizations," *The Review of Faith & International Affairs*, 6/4 (2008): 53-55 (53).

17. "BWA Responds to Letter from Muslim Leaders," *Good Faith Media*, website, January 6, 2009, https://goodfaithmedia.org/bwa-responds-to-letter-from-muslim-leaders-cms-13754/.

18. All the citations in this and the following paragraph come from the BWA letter, "From the Baptist World Alliance to the Muslim Leaders and Scholars who have written or signed *A Common Word Between Us and You*," available at https://www.acommonword.com/wp-content/uploads/2018/05/Extended_Response-Baptist_World_Alliance.pdf, accessed April 11, 2026.

19. "From the Baptist World Alliance to the Muslim Leaders and Scholars who have written or signed *A Common Word Between Us and You*."

20. "From the Baptist World Alliance to the Muslim Leaders and Scholars who have written or signed *A Common Word Between Us and You*."

21. Joint statement "A Declaration of Our Common Will," signed by the participants of the first North American Baptist-Muslim dialogue, on January 22, 2009, from the author's personal files.

22. Aliou Niang, "Loving God Whose Way Is Peace," *American Baptist Quarterly*, 31/3 (2012): 293-301 (294).

23. Niang, 297.

24. Niang, 300.

25. Karen Thomas Smith, *American Baptist Quarterly* 31/3 (2012): 346-347.

26. Description of the encounter shared among the dialogue's steering committee at the "Third National Baptist-Muslim Dialogue," item 4, from the author's personal files.

27. Ada María Isasi-Díaz, "Lo Cotidiano: A Key Element of Mujerista Theology," *Journal of Hispanic/Latino Theology,* 10/1 (2002): 5-17 (6).

28. Anthol Gill, "Human Rights: A Preliminary Sketch of 'A Down-Under Perspective'," *American Baptist Quarterly,* 9/4, 232-247 (232).

29. Luis Rivera-Pagán, "Reading the Hebrew Bible in Solidarity with the Palestinian People," in Raimundo C. Barreto, Jr., et al, eds., *Engaging the Jubilee: Freedom and Justice Papers of the Baptist World Alliance (2010-2015)* (Falls Church, Virginia: Baptist World Alliance, 2015), 102-125 (102).

30. Rivera-Pagán, 103.

31. Daniel L. Buttry, "Baptist Participation and Advocacy on Peace Issues in Our Global Context," in Raimundo C. Barreto, Jr, et al., eds., *Engaging the Jubilee: Freedom and Justice Papers of the Baptist World Alliance (2010-2015)* (Falls Church, Virginia: Baptist World Alliance, 2015), 300–307 (302).

32. R. Kirtie Algoe, "Christian-Muslim Relations in the Caribbean 1600-1900," in David Thomas and John Chesworth, eds., *Christian-Muslim Relations: A Bibliographical History* (Leiden: Brill, 2022), 481-491 (483).

33. Algoe, 484.

34. See Hendrik Kraemer, *The Christian Message in a Non-Christian World* (New York, NY: Harper & Brothers, 1938).

35. Joshua Kalapati, "Tambaram International Missionary Council Conference, 1938," in *The Oxford Encyclopaedia of South Asian Christianity* (Oxford, UK: Oxford University Press, 2011), Oxford Reference, website, https://www.oxfordreference.com/view/10.1093/acref/9780198073857.001.0001/acref-9780198073857-e-0961, accessed July 3, 2023.

36. M. M. Thomas, "An Assessment of Tambaram," *International Review of Mission*, 77/307 (1988): 390-397 (397).

37. Carlos F. Cardoza-Orlandi, "Inter-Religious Dialogue: Why Should It Matter to Our Academic and Grassroots Communities?" in Orlando O. Espín, ed., *The Wiley-Blackwell Companion to Latino/a Theology* (Malden, MA: Wiley-Blackwell, 2015), 475-491 (478).

38. Cardoza-Orlandi, 478.

39. See, for instance, Luiza E. Tomita, et al., eds. *Teologia Latino-Americana Pluralista da Libertação* (São Paulo: Paulinas, 2006).

40. Knitter, 10.

41. Arturo Escobar, *Designs for the Pluriverse* (Durham and London: Duke University Press, 2018), 148.

13. Loving Alike: A Wesleyan Vision for Interfaith Engagement

1. John Wesley, "Catholic Spirit," in *John Wesley's Sermons: An Anthology*, ed. Albert C. Outler and Richard P. Heitzenrater (Nashville: Abingdon Press, 1991), 301.

2. Paul D. Numrich, "Christian Sensitivity in Interreligious Relations," *The Asbury Journal* 67, no. 2 (2012): 53.

14. Interreligious Relations: An Evangelical Perspective

1. *Newsweek* (October 25, 1976), quoted by Jon Meacham, "The Editor's Desk," *Newsweek* website, November 12, 2006,

updated March 13, 2010, https://www.newsweek.com/editors-desk-42-106637.

2. For example, see dominion theology illustrated in the Seven Mountain Mandate of Johnny Enlow, *The Seven Mountain Prophecy: Unveiling the Coming Elijah Revolution* (Riverside, CA: Creation House, 2008); Johnny Enlow, *The Seven Mountain Mantle: Receiving the Joseph Anointing to Reform Nations* (Riverside, CA: Creation House, 2009); Lance Wallnau and Bill Johnson, *Invading Babylon: The 7 Mountain Mandate* (Shippensburg, PA: Destiny Image Publishers, 2013); Deborah McClendon, *Mandate to Invade the 7 Mountains of God: A Candid Look at Christianity's Influence on the 7 Spheres of Culture* (Scotts Valley, CA: CreateSpace Independent Publishing Platform, 2018); Robert Henderson, *Impacting the Seven Mountains from the Courts of Heaven: Kingdom Strategies for Revival in the Church and the Reformation of Culture* (Shippensburg, PA: Destiny Image, 2023); and Stephen Watathi, *The 7 Mountain Mandate: Strategy for Evangelizing the Modern World* (Independently Published, 2024).

3. "The Dangers of Christian Nationalism in the United States: A Policy Statement of the National Council of Churches," National Council of Churches website, April 20, 2021, https://nationalcouncilofchurches.us/common-witness/the-dangers-of-christian-nationalism-in-the-united-states-a-policy-statement-of-the-national-council-of-churches/.

4. Don Thorsen, *An Exploration of Christian Theology*, 2nd ed. (2008; Grand Rapids, Baker Academic, 2020), 290.

5. For example, see "Golden Rule," Living Peace International website, accessed September 28, 2025, http://livingpeaceinternational.org/en/the-project/regola-d-oro-2.html.

6. Luke 4:16b-21 provides a hybrid of Isaiah 61:1-2 and 58:6.

7. Although this saying has been attributed to Francis of Assisi, there is no historical evidence to substantiate it. Nevertheless, the sentiment reflects his emphasis on living the gospel through deeds, not just words.

16. The Middle East and Interfaith Relations: Intersections and Challenges

1. Shoulder to Shoulder, website, https://www.shouldertoshouldercampaign.org/vision, accessed April 2, 2026.

2. John McCain, quoted by Jonathan Martin and Amie Parnes, in "McCain: Obama Not an Arab, Crowd Boos," Politico, website, October 10, 2008, https://www.politico.com/story/2008/10/mccain-obama-not-an-arab-crowd-boos-014479.

3. Barack Obama, "Inaugural Address," January 21, 2009, https://obamawhitehouse.archives.gov/blog/2009/01/21/president-barack-obamas-inaugural-address.

17. Faith Beyond Boundaries: Reclaiming Pluralism in an Age of Christian Nationalism

1. Darrell Jodock and William Nelsen, *Embracing Diversity: Faith, Vocation, and the Promise of America* (Minneapolis: Fortress Press, 2021), 83.

2. Cf. Diana L. Eck, *A New Religious America: How a "Christian Country" Has Become the World's Most Religiously Diverse Nation* (New York: HarperCollins, 2001).

3. Andrew L. Whitehead and Samuel L. Perry, *Taking America Back for God: Christian Nationalism in the United States* (New York: Oxford University Press, 2022), 108.

4. Anastasios (Yannoulatos), *Coexistence: Peace, Nature, Poverty, Terrorism, Values (Religious Perspectives)*, trans. John Chryssavgis (Geneva: World Council of Churches, 2021), 81.

5. Anastasios (Yannoulatos), 17.

6. Cf. Peniel Jesudason Rufus Rajkumar and Joseph Prabhakar Dayam, eds., *Many Yet One: Multiple Religious Belonging* (Geneva: World Council of Churches, 2016), 1–4, and 45–61.

7. Cf. Joshua Samuel, "Practicing Multiple Religious Belonging for Liberation: A Dalit Perspective," *Current Dialogue* 55 (2015): 78–87.

8. Catholicos Aram I, "Our common calling" in *Changing the Present, Dreaming the Future: A Critical Moment in Interreligious Dialogue*, ed. Hans Ucko (Geneva: World Council of Churches, 2006), 14.

9. Raimon Panikkar, *The Intrareligious Dialogue* (New York: Paulist Press, 1999), 34–42.

10. Leonard Swidler, "The Dialogue Decalogue: Ground Rules for Interreligious, Interideological Dialogue" https://www.gvsu.edu/cms4/asset/843249C9-B1E5-BD47-A25EDBC68363B726/dialoguedecalogue.pdf.

11. National Council of the Churches of Christ in the USA Commission on Interfaith Relations, *Interfaith Relations and Christian Living: Study and Action Suggestions* (New York: National Council of Churches, 2000), 7.

12. Jodock and Nelson, 99-101.

13. Hans Ucko, ed., *Changing the Present, Dreaming the Future: A Critical Moment in Interreligious Dialogue* (Geneva: World Council of Churches, 2006), 80.

14. Cf. https://www.interfaithamerica.org/resources/pedagogies-for-pluralism/.

15. Ucko, 78.

16. Sonia P. Omulepu, ed., *Interfaith Education Initiative: A Manual on Interfaith Dialogue* (New York: Interfaith Education Initiative, n.d.), 58.

17. Ucko, 128.

18. How to Stay Human: Cruelty, Beauty, and Moral Leadership Today

1. Michael Reid Trice, *Encountering Cruelty: The Fracture of the Human Heart* (Leiden & Boston: Brill, 2011). The accounts of letters across millennia reveal much of human fear toward the neighbor. For example, see Sherry C. M. Lindquist and Asa Simon Mittman, *Medieval Monsters: Terrors, Aliens, Wonders* (New York: The Morgan Library & Museum, 2018).

2. James Davison Hunter, *Democracy and Solidarity: On the Cultural Roots of America's Political Crisis* (New Haven, CT: Yale University Press, 2024). See, particularly, the sections on personhood diminishment, a shrinking shared telos, and the rupture of authority and legitimacy.

3. Trice, *Encountering Cruelty.*

4. Václav Havel, "The Power of the Powerless," in *Open Letters: Selected Writings, 1965–1990* (New York: Vintage, 1992).

5. Friedrich Nietzsche, *On the Genealogy of Morals*, trans. Maudemarie Clark and Alan J. Swensen (Indianapolis: Hackett, 1998).

6. Nietzsche, *On the Genealogy of Morals.*

7. Albert Camus, *Reflections on the Guillotine*, trans. Richard Howard (New York: Vintage, 1959).

8. René Girard, *Deceit, Desire, and the Novel: Self and Other in Literary Structure*, trans. Yvonne Freccero (Baltimore: Johns Hopkins University Press, 1965); René Girard, *Violence and the Sacred*, trans. Patrick Gregory (Baltimore: Johns Hopkins University Press, 1977).

9. James Baldwin, *The Fire Next Time* (New York: Dial Press, 1963).

10. Much is written on the rise and requisite features of tyranny. Madeleine Albright's latest text is poignant as a warning. See, Madeleine Korbel Albright (with Bill Woodward), *Fascism: A Warning*, 1st ed. (New York: Harper, 2018).

11. Sacred wisdom disposes of an eye-for-an-eye across religious traditions, including in what may be ascribed as the handbook of Buddhist wisdom, *The Dhammapada*: "Hatred is never appeased by hatred. Hatred is appeased by love. This is an eternal law."

12. Wendell Berry, *The Art of the Commonplace: The Agrarian Essays of Wendell Berry*, ed. Norman Wirzba (Washington, DC: Counterpoint, 2002).

13. "My mercy encompasses all things," Qur'an 7:156

14. Thich Nhat Hanh, *The Art of Living: Peace and Freedom in the Here and Now* (New York: HarperOne, 2023): "We are here to awaken from the illusion of our separateness."

15. In the Western tradition, illuminated manuscripts of the Medieval period demonstrate the cosmological influence I have in mind. For a thrilling illustration see: Bryan C. Keene, ed., *Toward a Global Middle Ages: Encountering the World through Illuminated Manuscripts* (Los Angeles: J. Paul Getty Museum, 2019).

16. Martin Buber, *I and Thou*, trans. Walter Kaufmann (New York: Scribner, 1970).

17. This point is illustrated by existentialist author, Milan Kundera, *The Unbearable Lightness of Being*, trans. Michael Henry Heim (New York: Harper & Row, 1984). The protagonist, Sebina, reflects on beauty within the mass she encountered unexpectedly in the village church: "The mass was beautiful because it appeared to her in a sudden, mysterious revelation as a world betrayed." The world passing away renders its liturgy a precious albeit fleeting gift in time (p. 110).

18. Ronald A. Heifetz, Alexander Grashow, and Marty Linsky, *The Practice of Adaptive Leadership: Tools and Tactics for Changing Your Organization and the World* (Boston: Harvard Business Press, 2009).

19. Havel, "The Power of the Powerless."

20. This section owes much to Robin Wall Kimmerer, *Braiding Sweetgrass: Indigenous Wisdom, Scientific Knowledge, and the Teachings of Plants* (Minneapolis: Milkweed Editions, 2013).

21. Michael Reid Trice, "The First Council at Nicaea: Lessons from the Field," *Dialogue* (Winter 2024).

22. Trice, *Encountering Cruelty*.

23. Hannah Arendt, on evil's limitlessness/rootlessness, see *Eichmann in Jerusalem* (New York: Viking, 1963).

24. Sabbath as limit: Genesis 2:2-3; Exodus 20:8-11.